THE COMPLETE THINKER

DALE AHLQUIST

THE COMPLETE THINKER

The Marvelous Mind of
G. K. Chesterton

IGNATIUS PRESS   SAN FRANCISCO

Cover illustration by Ellen Price

Cover design by Riz Boncan Marsella

© 2012 by Ignatius Press, San Francisco
All rights reserved
ISBN 978-1-58617-675-4
Library of Congress Control Number 2012933884
Printed in the United States of America ∞

To the students of Chesterton Academy,
who were once only a figment of
my imagination but are now my
walking, talking, breathing, living inspiration.

CONTENTS

Acknowledgments   9

Introduction: "The Only Man I Regularly Read"   11

1. How to Think   21

2. Truth and Its Discontents   32

3. The Limits of Language   44

4. The Problem of Evil   55

5. The Seven Deadly Sins   65

6. The Universe and Other Little Things   86

7. Old and New   98

8. East and West   109

9. War and Peace   122

10. Politics and Patriotism   133

11. Law and Lawyers   147

12. Buying and Selling   160

13. Sickness and Health   180

14. Life and Death   195

15. Abandon Hopelessness, All Ye Who Enter Here   210

16. To Be   222

17. The Exception Proves the Rule   236

Appendix: Chesterton vs. Darrow   249

ACKNOWLEDGMENTS

Special thanks to the following fine folks for helping make this book happen: my wonderful wife, Laura, who has to read everything I write and is the only critic I care about; Stephen Beaumont, Chuck Chalberg, Kevin O'Brien, and the mighty crew at the Eternal Word Television Network (EWTN), who have helped make Chesterton come alive for millions; Peter Floriani, who has made my life and work easier, and who is also a complete thinker; Geir Hasnes, who keeps helping me find more Chesterton, and who is also a complete thinker; the editors, staff, and contributors to *Gilbert Magazine*, for offering a few good insights while cranking out the best magazine in the world; and the late great couple Frank and Ann Petta, for their unending encouragement and kindness. God rest their sweet souls.

INTRODUCTION

"The Only Man I Regularly Read"

I like to read myself to sleep in Bed,
A thing that every honest man has done
At one time or another, it is said,
But not as something in the usual run;
Now I from ten years old to forty one
Have never missed a night: and what I need
To buck me up is Gilbert Chesterton,
(The only man I regularly read).

The Illustrated London News is wed
To letter press as stodgy as a bun,
The Daily News might just as well be dead,
The "Idler" has a tawdry kind of fun,
The "Speaker" is a sort of Sally Lunn,
The "World" is like a small unpleasant weed;
I take them all because of Chesterton,
(The only man I regularly read).

The memories of the Duke of Beachy Head,
The memoirs of Lord Hildebrand (his son)
Are things I could have written on my head,
So are the memories of the Comte de Mun,
And as for novels written by the ton,
I'd burn the bloody lot! I know the Breed!
And get me back to be with Chesterton
(The only man I regularly read).

Prince, have you read a book called "Thoughts upon
The Ethos of the Athanasian Creed"?
No matter—it is not by Chesterton
(The only man I regularly read).

—Hilaire Belloc

I am sometimes asked if I ever read anything besides G. K.
Chesterton. The answer, unfortunately, is yes. I wish I had
a better answer—something more along the lines of no. It
would save me a lot of time and frustration if I did not
have to read other authors.

I am reminded of the warning in Ecclesiastes: "My son,
beware of anything beyond these. Of making many books
there is no end, and much study is a weariness of the flesh." [1]
What are the "these" in this passage? The sayings of the
wise, which the previous verse describes as "nails firmly
fixed", truths that do not change. It is indeed bothersome
to read anything else, when words of wisdom that already
sound good, simply because they ring with truth, sound even
better when the words themselves are melodious—as in the
quotations of G. K. Chesterton. When Chesterton says something so simple as: "To have a right to do a thing is not at
all the same as to be right in doing it", [2] we are immediately delighted with its truth, but we are also pleased by the
package it arrives in. A book-length treatise of the topic of
rights would not only be more painful and tiresome to read;
it would probably never get to such a clear and clean conclusion. This explains why I have been afflicted along with
many others who, after they have read Chesterton, are

---

[1] Ecclesiastes 12:12.
[2] G. K. Chesterton (hereafter, unless otherwise noted, the author is Chesterton), *A Short History of England*, in *The Collected Works of G. K. Chesterton*
(San Francisco: Ignatius Press, 2001), 20:505 (hereafter *CW*, followed by vol-
ume number and page number).

suddenly struck with a strange lack of desire to read any-body else. As one fellow sufferer said to me, "Chesterton sort of ruins other authors."

What is it that sets Chesterton apart, besides the fact that he is totally quotable? For one thing, he differs from some other outstanding literary figures of the last century in that he answers questions instead of just asking them. There are some fine artisans of the written word, skilled evokers of stirring and striking images, but their ideas are often disconnected, detached, and even decayed—a wilt that is lovely but suggests a lack of rootedness. Or, to switch metaphors, the fog they are lost in is sometimes interest-ing and eloquent, but it is still a fog and they are still lost in it. They express the problem very well—they write of the dilemma articulately—but they cannot find their way out. They do not have a solution. Their suggestiveness can only suggest.

But G. K. Chesterton is enormously clarifying. In an age of relativism, he speaks in absolutes. He speaks the truth without uncertainty, without wavering, and with-out embarrassment—and without the anger and pride that can befoul even the truth. He speaks with graciousness and goodness and humility. His epigrams ring with an instantly recognizable truth. But he does not merely sprinkle little encapsulated truths; he gushes with an ocean of truth. It is the whole truth. It is a comfort to most, a curiosity to some, and a curse to a few, but no honest reader can shake off the notion that Chesterton is consistently, extensively, and astonishingly right in what he writes.

And he writes about everything. I have been reading and studying and exploring Chesterton's writings for thirty years. He wrote more than just about any other writer in history, and I have read (and reread) most of it (no one has read all of it), and I can attest to the fact that there is almost no topic to which he has not at least made reference, usually provocatively, but always profoundly. And though I have dug deeply, I can also say that I feel like I am just *beginning* to discover Chesterton. I feel like I have just scratched the surface.

But Chesterton's great accomplishment is that, in addition to writing about everything, he puts it all together. He is a complete thinker. That is what this book is about.

The modern world tends toward specialization. It avoids generalization. There is an almost enforced fragmented thinking. Thus we have our academic disciplines, each sealed in its own department. One of the reasons Chesterton is not taught in most of our colleges and universities is that he is not narrow enough to fit into any one of their departments. He is larger than any of the available categories. But another reason he is not taught is that if he were given adequate treatment, there would be little time to teach anything else. Reading Chesterton is almost a complete education in itself. He informs every discipline. He opens doors from one thing to another and makes all the connections— whether it is the wonder at God's creation, which is the study of the natural sciences; the rigors of reason and logic, which is mathematics; the love of beauty and the provocation of imagination, which is art and literature; the passion for justice, which is law and politics; the challenge of getting our daily bread, which is economics; the search for meaning, which is philosophy; and the search for God and for all the truth that fills eternity, which is theology. Did I mention psychology? I wonder why not. Chesterton calls psychology "the mind studying the mind instead of studying the truth".[3]

---

[3] *New York American*, July 1, 1933.

Our fathers did not talk about psychology; they talked about a knowledge of Human Nature. But they had it; and we have not. They knew by instinct all the things we ignore by the help of information. For it is exactly the first facts about human nature that are now being ignored by humanity.[4]

It seems that one of Chesterton's main functions is to remind us of things we already know: common sense. "Every high civilization decays", warns Chesterton, "by forgetting obvious things."[5] What better description of the present state of our civilization? He prophetically points out that this decay includes a loss of respect for marriage, family, private property, and the value of life itself. He says human rights will be respected only when they are treated as divine rights.[6] But we are not allowed to discuss the divine origin of rights, or of life, or of existence. We are hardly allowed to discuss existence at all. And Chesterton asks, "If the ordinary man may not discuss existence, why should he be asked to conduct it?"[7]

It is a discussion that cannot be put off forever. "Nothing is important," says Chesterton, "except the fate of the soul."[8] There is, however, a real tension between those who take the fate of the soul seriously and those who do not. The conflict between religion and irreligion affects everything else in our society. The two sides need to start talking. In fact, they need to do more than talk. They need to argue: "The aim of argument is differing in order to agree; the failure of argument is when you agree to differ."[9]

---

[4] *Sidelights*, *CW* 21:505.

[5] *The New Jerusalem*, *CW* 20:211.

[6] *Illustrated London News* (hereafter *ILN*), January 13, 1912.

[7] *George Bernard Shaw*, *CW* 11:482.

[8] *Appreciations and Criticisms of the Works of Charles Dickens*, *CW* 15:271.

[9] *ILN*, April 1, 1911.

There will be some arguing in this book. You will find me taking Chesterton's side in these arguments. It is not because I have never considered the other side, but because I have. I have myself argued with Chesterton, and each time I have been gloriously defeated. But also, I have considered some of the other people who have argued with Chesterton. I have noticed not only the bankruptcy of their ideas but the emptiness of their lives. Neither they nor their arguments hold up well against the Wild Knight of Battersea, the Laughing Prophet of Beaconsfield.

There will be some who will scoff at this book as not being "critical" enough of Chesterton. But Chesterton's critics are on the whole a sorry lot, and I do not wish to be counted among their sad number. They excel in what Chesterton calls the art of missing the point. But most of them are simply small (as are Shakespeare's critics; see chapter 16). Their criticisms are really not worth mentioning, and yet they are always mentioned when Chesterton's name comes up. I reluctantly mention them now. The sometimes baffling list includes the charges that Chesterton was an anti-Semite, a racist, a misogynist, a homosexual (or, even more alarmingly, a *repressed* homosexual), a sado-masochist, a glutton, a drunk, a reactionary, a socialist, a right-winger, a radical, a malleable immature misfit who was careless with the real facts and wasteful of his real talent, if he had any. The reason these are not worth mentioning is that they are not true. They are sometimes dressed up as criticisms, but they are all designed to do one thing: dismiss Chesterton, to do away with him without considering his ideas.

I am not saying that Chesterton cannot be criticized. I am only saying that I have never seen it done creditably or convincingly. And I have read all of the criticisms. Time wasted. I could have been reading Chesterton. In every case, the criticisms have always revealed more about the critics than they have about Chesterton.

There is no need to defend Chesterton. And he would agree. He is never concerned with defending himself, only with defending the truth. Interestingly enough, his first book of essays was called *The Defendant*, in which he defends things that were not properly appreciated in the modern world—like babies.

Chesterton's problem is not his critics. It is the literary and academic establishment that has overlooked or ignored him, passing over him in favor of his contemporaries: Thomas Hardy, George Bernard Shaw, James Joyce, W. B. Yeats, and others whose literary brilliance is marked by doubt or despair or cynical detachment. Students are thus served up a thin fare of narrow views and broken ideas. Missing from the syllabus is a beautiful writer who is also a complete thinker.

It is possible that Chesterton is neglected for practical reasons. By simply avoiding his writings, we do not have to trouble ourselves with the cumbersome matter of Chesterton's Catholic faith. In fact, that alone provides some academics with motivation for dismissing him out of hand. But even if we leave religion out of it, the fact is, we really do not want to deal with a complete thinker. It is not efficient.

And where has such efficiency led us?

> [This] is the chief practical result of modern practical orga-
> nization and efficiency. The division of labour has become
> the division of mind; and means in a new and sinister sense
> that the right hand does not know what the left hand doeth.
> In an age of universal education, nobody knows where any-
> thing comes from. The process of production has become
> so indirect, so multitudinous and so anonymous, that to

trace anything to its origin is to enter upon sort of detective story, or the exploration of a concealed crime.[10]

Chesterton's concealed crime is that he really believed the Catholic creed in all its fullness. The concealed crime is that there is no crime. The deeper we dig into Chesterton's life and works, the more we discover hidden virtues instead of hidden vices. Yet, in spite of Chesterton's vast intellectual reach, he has been shelved for being narrow-minded, while skeptics are hailed for being broad-minded. However, the truth is precisely the other way around: "Men will not believe because they will not broaden their minds."[11]

We can learn from Chesterton not only how to be a complete thinker but how to argue with our adversaries. He is the model of calm and reason and good humor, not only because he is confident about the truth, but because he cares about the souls of his opponents. He wants to win them over because he loves them, not because he merely wants to prove that he is right. He always sees the connection between truth and charity. It is part of his completeness.

But what is a complete thinker?

First of all, complete thinking means grasping the hierarchy of knowledge, that is, thinking important thoughts, the most important thoughts, the highest and best thoughts. From this elevated perspective, as it were, we see how everything else fits together.

Secondly, it means thinking worthwhile thoughts, thoughts that are literally worth our time—the most limited commodity that we have. Thinking should not be a waste of time. It should be the most productive and fruitful use of our time, leading to worthwhile actions that reflect our thinking.

[10] *G. K.'s Weekly*, June 14, 1930.
[11] *St. Francis of Assisi*, *CW* 2:36.

Thirdly, it means knowing how to fill in the blanks, that is, how to fill the gaps of our knowledge. We cannot know everything, but we can connect what we do know with coherence.

Fourthly, it means making the most of both faith and reason, demonstrating that they do not contradict one another and can be used to test everything that calls itself the truth. "Men have always one of two things: either a complete and conscious philosophy or the unconscious acceptance of the broken bits of some incomplete and shattered and often discredited philosophy." [12]

Although Chesterton writes about everything, he makes this striking claim: "There is only one subject." [13] There is one central truth, to which all other truths are connected, and which is under attack from all sides by error, by mistakes, by foolishness, by sin. Chesterton understands that in defending this truth he has to be prepared to talk about everything. And so that is what he talks about—everything. He is also willing to argue, to fight. "If you are loyal to anything and wish to preserve it, you must recognize that it has or might have enemies; and you must hope that the enemies will fail." [14]

For the last three decades, I have enjoyed not only taking an active role in the Chesterton revival, but simply watching it as well. The greatest privilege has been watching the endless parade of Chesterton's words march by and present themselves for inspection, watching the wheels of his great mind turn as he considers the truth that touches everything, watching the winds of his great soul blow away all the intellectual garbage and strange and horrible ideas that

---

[12] *The Common Man* (New York: Sheed and Ward, 1950), 173.
[13] *ILN*, February 17, 1906.
[14] *ILN*, July 29, 1911.

clutter the modern world, and watching his sure hand as he defends the faith that changed his life, the faith that changed my life. There is a reason he writes with such strength and assurance. As he points out, "faith" and "confidence" are derived from the same word: *fides*. Chesterton is a giant of the faith, and a model of confidence in the truth. He puts it all together.

I invite you to come with me now and take a brief but scenic tour of the mind of a complete thinker.

How to Think

If people must not be taught religion, they might be taught reason, philosophy. If the State must not teach them to pray it might teach them to think. And when I say that children should be taught to think I do not mean (like many moderns) that they should be taught to doubt; for the two processes are not only not the same, but are in many ways opposite. To doubt is only to destroy; to think is to create.

—*Daily News*, June 22, 1907

When the prevailing philosophy claims that truth is relative or basically unknowable or strictly personal or largely irrelevant, in other words, when our only certainty is our uncertainty, there is nothing more irritating than someone coming along and smashing such nonconclusive conclusions. There is nothing more unsettling than someone who has settled things. The most unwelcome person on a college campus today is someone who can argue persuasively that there is a truth that is absolute, all-important, accessible, and universal. This partly explains why G. K. Chesterton is not taught or studied or even considered in most of our universities.

Of course, he also violates almost every tenet of political correctness. Go right down the list: he criticizes feminism, vegetarianism, modern art (starting from Impressionism), free verse, pornography, immorality, contraception, compulsory education, and loud music in restaurants. He defies the gods: Darwin, Marx, Freud, and Nietzsche. He even criticizes James Joyce.

But these are details. It is not what he attacks but what he defends that keeps him outside the guarded fortresses of higher education. He defends marriage. He defends having babies. He defends Western civilization. He defends the Crusades. He defends the Catholic Church. If that is not bad enough, he even defends smoking.

His balanced attacks, however, throw everyone off balance: he criticizes both socialism *and* capitalism, both big government *and* big business, both liberals *and* conservatives. He also criticizes paganism *and* puritanism; optimists *and* pessimists; and even coffee, tea, *and* cocoa—they "awaken but do not stimulate", and they never have produced any good drinking songs.[1]

But in spite of all these apparent disadvantages, it is G. K. Chesterton who has the advantage over his adversaries. He is bigger than they are. You may think I am referring to the three-hundred-pounder who called himself the politest man in England because he could stand up on a bus and offer his seat to three women at once. No, I am talking about the fact that he created something even bigger than himself: an incredible and incalculable body of writing that seems to cover *everything* and reveals G. K. Chesterton as that rarest of all human birds—a complete thinker. His opponents suffer from the problem of being not merely small but narrow: they may disagree with Chesterton on the point

---

[1] *New York American*, April 10, 1935.

that affects them or about the issue that concerns them the most, but all they offer is that one point or that single issue; they do not demonstrate any thought beyond that. Feminists cannot get past their feminism. Socialists cannot get past their socialism. Capitalists cannot get past their capitalism. Evolutionists cannot get past their cells. Psychologists cannot get past their pasts. They are all of them almost comically obsessed with the small thing that defines them. Chesterton cannot even be defined. He cannot be pigeonholed. Our categories are too small to hold him. And so we have the irony of a three-hundred-pound writer who has fallen through the cracks.

The problem, of course, is not with Chesterton, but with our compartmentalized way of thinking and our departmentalized way of teaching. In the modern world, everything is separated from everything else. It is evident everywhere, but especially in our schools.

> The present collapse of this country began with ... the first time when Education was substituted for culture ... [when] instruction was regarded as a substitute for education ... [when] men had begun only to get facts by teaching and not truth by tradition. For the facts were few, were carefully selected, were almost always trivial. They were, in short, the facts now taught by the new power of Compulsory Education.[2]

The true goal of education should be continuity, preserving what has been learned from one generation to the next, rather than neglecting tradition and ignoring the past. It is a primary part of a parent's duty to keep the culture going. "A Culture", says Chesterton, "is a thing complete of its kind; that is, it covers the field of life and the ways of

[2] *G. K.'s Weekly*, August 27, 1932.

this world somehow; it has some version of everything; it can give some account of itself in dealing with anything." [3] But if everything is separated from everything else, and if the central truth that holds everything together is purposely avoided, then it is not surprising that we have a divided society, one that cannot give a uniform account of itself and must try new educational experiments on a regular basis because many students fail to master even fundamental subjects.

Thinking is a skill. Like any skill, it can be taught. It is a simple skill, but it is still hard work. In fact, Chesterton says that thinking is the hardest work in the world. And hard work, he says, is repugnant to our nature. [4]

We are lazy. And we would rather have someone else do our work for us. We do not fight for ourselves; we do not entertain ourselves; we do not govern ourselves. We do not even think for ourselves. It is much easier to have someone else tell us what to think.

One of the reasons it is hard to think is that it is hard to talk. It is hard work to put our thoughts into actual words. Even when we put language to work, we find that language is always falling short of what we want it to do. Chesterton says, "We are struggling in a fallen language like men struggling inside the folds of a fallen tent." [5]

And it seems as if language continues to fall. It is hard to imagine how much further it can fall. We seem to be getting more and more inarticulate. We try to say more and more with fewer and fewer words. If you want a really horrifying vision of the future, just take a look at the way our young people talk. How many times have you heard variations of the following? "Like, you know, um, he's like looking at me,

[3] Ibid.
[4] See *ILN*, September 26, 1914.
[5] *ILN*, December 24, 1910.

you know, and I'm, um, like: 'What are you looking at me for?' And you know he's like, um, 'I'm not looking at you', and I'm, um, like, you know, 'It looks like you're like looking at me.' And he's like you know, 'Like, why would I look at you?' and I'm like, 'Whatever!'"

They have taken this form of minimalist language to its minimum. Their vocabulary consists mostly of "like", "um", and "you know".

Perhaps the only word with multiple syllables that you will hear them say is "whatever", the ultimate postmodern word. It reveals the thinking of the postmodern world—well, not the thinking, but the default position, which is, "I'm not going to think about this."

What do those other words mean?

"Like" means a lack of precision; it means only an approximation, a vague similarity. They cannot say what "is", only what is "like". They cannot even say "say". "Like" has replaced "say".

What does "you know" mean? "You know" means "*I don't* know." It means "I hope *you* know because I don't. I don't know what I'm saying, because I haven't figured out how to say it or even what to say. You know?"

What does "um" mean? "Um" sums up everything else that is missing from their vocabulary and their minds. It is just a sound that is utterly meaningless. And yet it takes up the greater part of their speech.

But why can't they talk? Because they cannot think. There are no words because there are no thoughts that correspond with them. And why can't they think? Because we have not taught them how to think.

And what could be more frustrating for them? They get angry because they cannot express their anger, because they cannot express anything. Finally the rage is released in the most brutal and unimaginable ways—in loud pounding music that fills their empty heads with sound instead of words, in loveless sex that fills their empty souls with something like a substitute for affection, or, ultimately and tragically, in something even worse: in death, violent death, in the murder of their unborn children, of their fellow students, or of themselves.

Yes, thinking is important. Chesterton says, "If you think wrong, you go wrong." [6] That is why we need to be taught how to think.

Thinking could be taught in our schools today. It was taught in medieval schools and could be taught quite easily again. Most thinking, says Chesterton, consists of a few quite elementary maxims.[7] This basic equipment, these simple tests, would save us a lot of trouble and a lot of work. Let's take them one at a time:

1. All proof begins with something which cannot be proved, but can only be perceived or accepted, and is called an axiom or first principle.

"Faith precedes all argument", says Chesterton. This is a point laid down in Euclid. "Euclid ... cannot prove one proposition without getting us to agree in his assumptions." [8]

You cannot prove an assumption; you can only assume it. But you cannot reason without it. Even Father Brown, Chesterton's great detective and problem solver, affirms this: "Only a man who knows nothing of reason talks of reasoning without strong, undisputed first principles." [9]

Here is a basic, undisputed first principle; Chesterton realized it when he was a young man. He was struggling with

[6] *ILN*, September 12, 1914.
[7] See *ILN*, July 10, 1915.
[8] *Daily News* (hereafter *DN*), July 16, 1904.
[9] "The Blue Cross", in *The Innocence of Father Brown*, *CW* 12:35.

depression and was really quite deep in a personal darkness, but he grasped one rudimentary first principle that helped pull him out of it, and this was long before he embraced Christianity. It was this: existence is better than nonexistence.

> I invented a rudimentary and makeshift mystical theory of my own. It was substantially this; that even mere existence, reduced to its most primary limits, was extraordinary enough to be exciting. Anything was magnificent as compared with nothing.[10]

If we start with that idea, we can do a lot of good thinking, and we can avoid a lot of bad thinking.

2. There can be no argument except between those who accept the same first principle.

Chesterton could debate with anyone because he could always find something he agreed with in his opponent's argument, and then by building on that common ground he would proceed to demonstrate the incompleteness of his opponent's argument.

There was only one person Chesterton refused to debate—a Satanist, a man with whom he could find nothing in common, no first principles. I have called Chesterton the Apostle of Common Sense because of his great ability to appeal to truths that we all recognize to be true, that is, to the truths we have in common. There are exceptions, of course. There are people who reject even the common truths. But if we cannot agree on first principles, such as "existence is better than non-existence", then we really cannot hold a conversation, not even about the weather.

3. An act can only be judged by defining its object.

[10] *Autobiography, CW* 16:96.

One of the reasons we do not know how to think is that we cannot define the object of our actions. Chesterton says, "The whole of modern civilization ... does not know what it is trying to find; and therefore does not find it." [11]

If we say that existence is better than nonexistence, what is the object of existence? Chesterton's answer: "The only object of existence is to mean something." [12]

> All through history, there have been broad conceptions of the aims of life, tests of morality which masses of men have held and applied with certainty; but in the modern world these various systems have been abandoned and what is left of them is nothing but debris—a collection of broken bits, the ruins of past philosophies. There are some, like myself, who hold a mystical philosophy, a belief that behind human experience there are realities, powers of good and evil, and the final test for things is their influence for good or evil. The good power intends us to be happy and we are justified in being happy, but the real question is not whether we are happy, but whether, behind the things wherein we seek our happiness lies the power of good. Are they parts of the good or of the evil? [13]

Everyone wants happiness. But can we be happy with evil? Is there a higher test than just happiness? Where are we going? Can we choose to go there or must we go there?

Most modern ideas about human behavior are deterministic. They rob us of our free will. Our actions and their consequences are explained by biology or psychology or sociology or economics or sex or the mood we were in

---

[11] *The Spice of Life* (Philadelphia: DuFour Editions, 1966), 9.

[12] *ILN*, November 11, 1905.

[13] "The Need of a Philosophy", *The Philosopher* 1 (1923), report of a lecture, March 7, 1923.

that day. Chesterton points out that if we take any of these modern philosophies to their logical conclusions, they lead to madness and then self-destruction. A strict determinist cannot even say, "Please pass the salt."

The attack on free will, on personal responsibility, has also diminished our ability to think for ourselves. It has even left us despairing of thinking we should think for ourselves. Only with free will are we able to enjoy the freedom to pursue joy. And that is why existence is better than nonexistence.

And so, these three maxims are essential; they form the basis by which we can test anything: What are its origins, and what are its ends? What are the first principles? Can we agree on them enough to argue? And what is our ultimate goal?

If we follow these three maxims, we would know how to think. There is another way to learn how to think: to follow the example of a great thinker. There are few things that give a better appreciation of everything than watching a great mind at work. For some reason, the mind of G. K. Chesterton comes to mind.

Chesterton begins at the beginning: creation. Everything could not have come from nothing. When we acknowledge God as the Creator, we see everything else in its proper perspective. Chesterton realizes that existence itself is a gift, something we did not deserve. The only appropriate response to a gift is gratitude. He says, "Thanks are the highest form of thought." [14] If we fill our day with thankfulness, we will eliminate most of the anger and frustration and distraction we contribute to the world's overall confusion.

The next point is that God made us in his own image. This is the basis of the dignity of all human beings. But it

[14] *A Short History of England, CW* 20:463.

also means that we, too, are creators. This is the basis of all art. Just as we are mirrors of God, so our creations are mirrors of us, further reflecting God's glory like a giant, brilliant, multifaceted diamond.

But the mirror is broken. There is a major disconnect between God and us. The broken connection is called sin. Chesterton is an "original" thinker because he emphasizes Original Sin. He says it is the only Christian doctrine that we can prove.[15] Just look around. There is a created order, and in keeping that order, we are happy, and we are free. In upsetting that order, we inflict a disorder that makes us miserable. And the whole world is very miserable.

But there is a way out of this misery, a solution so creative it could only have come from the Creator himself. It is what Chesterton calls "The Strangest Story in the World",[16] the story of God sacrificing himself to himself, of turning his back on himself, of dying a horrible death because of the horrible sin in the world, but defeating death by rising from the dead. The story of Jesus Christ is either the fundamental truth of existence or else it is the most fabulous lie in history. But if it is true, it affects everything else: "Things can be irrelevant to the proposition that Christianity is false, but nothing can be irrelevant to the proposition that Christianity is true."[17]

When Christ came, he did not found a new religion; he did not start an ethical society, but established something else completely different: a Church. That Church built our civilization. It brought us the sacraments; it gave authority to the law and balanced justice with mercy and took care of the poor and chastised the rich and celebrated the

---

[15] See "The Maniac", in Orthodoxy, CW 1:217.
[16] See the chapter of this title in The Everlasting Man, CW 2:331–45.
[17] DN, December 12, 1903.

marriages and blessed the babies and buried the dead, and the world has turned around and robbed it, ridiculed it, and reduced its role in society. But the gates of hell have not prevailed against it. The Catholic Church, says Chesterton, is not merely right, but right where everything else is wrong.[18] And that is why this amazingly profound and clear thinker, G. K. Chesterton, chose to join that Church and said, "To become a Catholic is not to leave off thinking, but to learn how to think." [19]

Think about it.

---

[18] See *The Thing*, *CW* 3:190.
[19] *The Catholic Church and Conversion*, *CW* 3:106.

2

Truth and Its Discontents

We are not entitled to despair of explaining the truth; nor is it really so horribly difficult to explain.

—*The Thing*

Many people do not like paradoxes. They do not like truth being more complicated than what they expect, or, as is more often the case, *less* complicated than what they expect. In other words, they do not like truth being anything other than what they expect. And that is precisely the problem with paradox: it is a truth that is unexpected.

Now why is it that truth should come as something unexpected? There is only one answer to that question, as obvious as it is troubling. Truth is unexpected because we have come to expect something other than the truth. And if it is not the truth, it is one of two things: it is an error, which can sometimes be quite innocent, or it is a lie, which is never innocent.

One of the strangest trends of the technological age is that the less we trust people, the more we trust machines. We put actors on camera, but we put cameras on employees. We almost expect politicians to lie to us, but we always expect machines to tell us the truth. The electronic authority of television is now being transferred to computers, but both have the newspaper as their forefather. The words and images that now rush through the Internet, once rushed across the airwaves, and before that rushed onto the printed page, words that seem so urgent, but disappear in a day. It is as fitting as it is fabulous that G. K. Chesterton made his living as a journalist, that his throwaway words survive, that his observations still hit the mark. In fact, what he says about the newspapers is even more true of our electronic media: "Modern man is staggering and losing his balance because he is being pelted with little pieces of alleged fact which is native to the newspapers; and, if they turn out not to be facts, that is still more native to the newspapers." [1] He knows how easy it is for the news media to twist the truth, to conceal the truth, to deny the truth, or simply to neglect the truth. He knows, too, that the reliability of machines can only go so far. This is explained by a fictional priest named Father Brown: "No machine can lie, nor can it tell the truth.... You always forget that the reliable machine always has to be worked by an unreliable machine ... I mean Man ... the most unreliable machine I know of." [2]

The other place where we should expect to find the truth, but are in fact surprised if we do find it, is the classroom of a college or university. The main problem is that the pervasive philosophy at these institutions is that truth is relative, that we dare not even make any pronouncements about it. What is worse is that we cannot even debate about it. The idea behind debate is to describe the truth by attempting to defend it, to discover the truth by attempting to deny

[1] *ILN*, April 7, 1923.
[2] "The Mistake of the Machine", in *The Wisdom of Father Brown*, *CW* 12:313.

it—to argue about it. But in much of the modern world—in politics and education and in the public square—there is no real debate. There is the occasional shouting match, the exchange of catchwords, the sneering and sloganeering and silencing. There is certainly no debate at all with someone who is holding a bomb. But neither is there any debate with someone who is holding a government or a newspaper or a television station. And there is no debate with someone who is holding a university.

To claim that anything is the truth—the moral or philosophical or theological truth—is to open oneself to attack. But for anyone who cares about the truth, that should be when the fun starts. It is a pleasure to have our ideas put to the test. The battle is thrilling.

The casual critic is always ready to proclaim that some philosophy is false or some statement is misleading or some idea is crazy; but while he is ready to attack, he is slow to defend. He does not dare declare that a metaphysical proposition is the truth. He does not even dare suggest it. But how can we point out what is wrong, if we are unwilling to say what is right? As Chesterton says, "In order to suppress false doctrine, we must have a definition of true doctrine." [3]

But as soon as we make a bold statement about the truth, we can expect one of three standard objections; Chesterton has a response for each.

1.   "Truth is unknowable."

You cannot take the region called the unknown and calmly say that though you know nothing about it, you know that all its gates are locked. . . . We do not know enough about the unknown to know that it is unknowable.[4]

---

[3] *ILN*, March 23, 1929.
[4] *William Blake* (London: House of Stratus, 2000), 21.

In order to know the truth it is necessary to desire the truth, especially the truth that you do not know.[5]

2.   "We cannot know the whole truth. We can only know aspects of the truth."

If we talk of a certain thing being an aspect of truth, it is evident that we claim to know what is truth; just as, if we talk of the hind leg of a dog, we claim to know what is a dog.[6]

3.   "Truth is relative."

If truth is relative, to what is it relative?[7]

Chesterton's quotations are concentrated doses of truth, amazing zingers that work like ammunition to shoot down doubts. And while their truth is self-evident and self-contained, they spring from one basic principle that Chesterton applies to religion, to education, to scientific inquiry, to medicine, to law and politics and debate, and to great art and literature. That one principle is simply this: "that there is a whole truth of things, and that in knowing it and speaking it we are happy." [8] No matter what we are studying, what we are pursuing, what we are doing, there is a right order, a right way of thinking, a right way of doing things, and if we fall short of the truth, we will be frustrated and unfulfilled.

Truth is not something that we can make up. It exists in spite of us. Though Chesterton is a great defender of democracy, truth is not a matter of what the majority has decided. He says, "Democracy is right when it stands for the normal;

[5] DN, October 19, 1907.
[6] Heretics, CW 1:200.
[7] DN, June 2, 1906.
[8] ILN, August 11, 1906.

not when it stands for the average." [9] There is another term for the normal: common sense.

But we have become almost as afraid to say what normal is as to say what truth is. We are afraid of being accused of intolerance or fanaticism. But this is backwards. It is the accusers who are intolerant and fanatical. For instance, Chesterton points out that the strangest fanaticism that fills our time "is the fanatical hatred of morality, especially of Christian morality." [10]

We do not live in a truth-seeking age. We live in a pleasure-seeking age. With pleasure as our goal, we are destined for disappointment. "The very fury with which people go on seeking pleasure is a proof that they have not found it." [11]

After the three standard knee-jerk objections are parried, there remains the real challenge flung into the face of truth: How do you know it is the truth? We should not be intimidated by this question. There are at least five tests that the truth must pass in order to establish itself as the truth. And Chesterton is proficient at all five.

First of all, truth is consistent. The glory days of great debate were about two thousand years ago in Rome. And one of the great debaters was Seneca. He said, *Veritas in omnem sui partem eadem est*. The rough English translation (and all English translations are a little rough) is, "Truth is always the same in all its parts." In other words, truth is consistent. A liar has a hard time keeping his story straight. A false philosophy cannot be maintained; at some point it is compromised by reality. A man who is in error will find that his argument simply does not hold up.

[9] *DN*, February 25, 1911.
[10] *A Handful of Authors* (New York: Sheed and Ward, 1953), 66.
[11] *Sidelights*, *CW* 21:503.

Chesterton is, if nothing else, consistent. One of the most astonishing things about his writing is how it is all of a piece. It can sometimes be impossible to date, but it is always recognizable as being Chesterton. He is always defending the same position, always making the same points, whether he is writing a newspaper column, a poem, a literary biography, or a murder mystery, whether he is writing in 1901 or in 1931. Toward the end of his life, Chesterton was accused of saying nothing new, to which he of course pled guilty, but he was puzzled as to why this should be considered a meaningful criticism.

Secondly, truth does not change. This is consistent with truth being consistent. When Chesterton was accused of believing things that "may have been true in the twelfth century but can't possibly be true in the twentieth century", he responded that this was like saying it was all right to believe something on Tuesday but not on Wednesday.[12] The point is that truth does not depend on the day of the week; it does not depend on the century; it does not depend on the millennium. Truth does not wear out. Fads and fashions and movements wear out. They come and they go. Truth survives movements and moods and manias. "The fact that a chaotic and ill-educated time cannot clearly grasp the truth does not alter the fact that it always will be the truth."[13]

Thirdly, truth is distinctive. A lie is a form of camouflage. It is an attempt to make the background as important as the foreground, to emphasize what is unimportant—and also to de-emphasize what is important, even to lose it altogether. In a world of lies we are unable or unwilling to see anything against a background of everything else. Chesterton is always trying to draw attention to the outline of truth,

[12] *Orthodoxy, CW* 1:278.
[13] *ILN*, March 23, 1929.

the thing that sets it apart from everything that it is not. And this is both an artistic principle and a philosophical one. As he says, "Art, like morality, consists of drawing the line somewhere." [14]

Fourthly, along with truth's consistency and changelessness and distinctiveness is its wholeness. Anything less than the truth is a heresy. A heresy is a selection of part of the truth that results in the rejection of the rest of it. A heresy is a lie because every half-truth is a lie. Most heresies are less than half the truth. But the point is that a heresy means not being satisfied with the whole truth; it means thinking our own version of the truth in its truncated form is more important than truth in its entirety.

Chesterton uses the striking and straightforward word "heretic" to describe most modern thinkers. As we know, he even wrote a book about it. His point is that heretics are monomaniacs—they are obsessively focused on partial truths and neglectful of the whole truth. "The whole truth is generally the ally of virtue; a half-truth is always the ally of some vice." [15]

This brings me to the fifth and most important characteristic of truth: truth is good. Even though this should be obvious, it still needs to be said. Though the fact that it needs to be said shows that it is not obvious, because, in a sinful world, truth is paradoxical. Truth is not obvious. The good, for some reason, gets very little publicity. The good is unpopular. And yet we *know* truth is good. The corollary is that error is bad. And Chesterton adds, "If large numbers of nice people are held captive by error that is all the more reason for destroying the error and setting them free." [16]

---

[14] *ILN*, May 5, 1928.
[15] *ILN*, June 11, 1920.
[16] *DN*, March 26, 1910.

The promise of Christ still rings across the millennia: the truth will set us free.[17] We are drawn to the truth the way any slave is drawn to freedom. But we resist the truth the way any slave is unwilling to risk the danger of escape. Slavery is easy. Freedom is hard. But we know which is the better state. "Though we are all liars, we all love the truth."[18]

Truth makes us uncomfortable because we know we are sinners. People may tell lies for what they think is their own good, but it is only for their own advantage. And advantage is not good because it means someone else is at a disadvantage. A lie is uncharitable. A lie does no one any good, least of all the person who tells it. It is destructive, but mostly self-destructive. Chesterton shows us the distinction between our motives in telling a lie or telling the truth: "The object of telling the truth is that you may be believed afterwards. The object of telling a lie is that you may be believed now."[19]

Truth is good. All the virtues are good, and all the virtues are tied together. But, as Chesterton points out, we have separated the virtues from each other.[20] In our broken system the virtues are at war so that wisdom and charity fight each other, patience and courage are at odds, humility and fortitude refuse to appear together.

G. K. Chesterton affirms what is good. Whether it is something so simple as making a child laugh or the more difficult task of making a jaded adult laugh, whether it is defending the simple good of helping a man quench his thirst or the more profound good of helping a man own his own property, whether it is describing something of temporal importance like a just society or something of eternal

[17] See John 8:32.
[18] *ILN*, March 14, 1908.
[19] *ILN*, October 24, 1914.
[20] See *Orthodoxy, CW* 1:233.

importance like man finding peace with God, the Maker of all good things, Chesterton affirms what is good and what is true. Moreover, Chesterton himself is a man of virtue. His gratitude and his humility and his joy reveal his goodness and his truthfulness. It also makes him unafraid to speak the truth.

Even though truth is good, there are people who prefer a vague idea of what is good to a very clear idea of what is true. They do not want to take a stand for the truth, because, well, somebody might disagree—or get offended. As noted above, speaking the truth can get us into a fight. Some people are under the impression that a fight is unpleasant, but there is one part of a fight that should be pleasing. It should be exhilarating to defend what we love. Paradoxically, a fight for what is true is actually an act of love.

But truth is to be enjoyed and not just defended. Truth is precious. It is like a rare jewel. Lies are cheap—and legion. Lies are recognizable by their very abundance—like weeds. Chesterton says, "Truth is sacred; and if you tell the truth too often nobody will believe it." [21] Unfortunately, the same cannot be said for the common falsehoods of modern thought. The more they are repeated, the more they are believed.

What is perhaps even more pernicious than outright lies is simply the lack of definition, the muddiness about the truth that encourages doubt and discourages faith. One of the great modern fallacies is that doubt, or skepticism, is somehow more profound and more honest and more intellectually pure than belief. But it turns out that doubt is usually reactionary and shallow and prejudicial and inconsistent. We cannot build a philosophy based on doubt. We cannot build anything that is based only on tearing something else down.

[21] *ILN*, February 24, 1906.

But it is doubt that has led the way in the modern world. It is doubt that lies at the heart of one particular false virtue, one broken stance, one shifting foundation that is always preferred to truth in today's world. It goes by the name "tolerance". But even the name is false. True tolerance means bearing with a person with whom we disagree. We cannot have tolerance unless we first disagree with our opponent. But tolerance in today's parlance silences disagreement. Chesterton exposes such tolerance on all its flanks.

> Those who merely denounce intolerance seem to have no theory at all with which to defend toleration.[22]

> The modern idea is that cosmic truth is so unimportant that it cannot matter what anyone says.[23]

> Everyone's belief is everyone else's concern.[24]

> Those who talk of "tolerating all opinions" are very provincial bigots who are only familiar with one opinion.[25]

> Men are never so mean and false and hypocritical as when they are occupied in being impartial.[26]

> Impartiality ... is the most irritating thing I can think of.[27]

Impartiality, says Chesterton, is only "a pompous name for indifference".[28] Perhaps the most famous indifferent person in history was Pontius Pilate, a man who was unwilling to make a decision, unwilling to get his hands dirty; a man who thought it was safe to hide behind the question, "What

[22] *ILN*, June 9, 1923.
[23] *Heretics*, *CW* 1:41.
[24] *ILN*, September 6, 1913.
[25] *ILN*, February 24, 1912.
[26] *What I Saw in America*, *CW* 21:244.
[27] *Sidelights*, *CW* 21:503.
[28] *The Speaker*, December 15, 1900.

is truth?" As Chesterton says, Pontius Pilate "showed his taste for epigram at a somewhat unlikely moment." [29]

He also refers to the infamous question in this charming episode:

> A little boy was sitting on my knee the other day while I was reading a new book of philosophy. He could just read capital letters, and he read across the top of a chapter "What is truth?" And the moment he saw this grey and ironical riddle of old Pontius Pilate, he called out in a sudden shrill and exultant voice, "Oh, that is an easy question. I know what truth is. It's saying things right." And so indeed it is; that is the best answer to the question, except the colossal silence of Christ. But the point here is, that the whole strength of the child lay not in the fact that he solved the difficulty, but that he did not admit that there was any difficulty.[30]

Truth is "saying things right". But still: What is truth? Pontius Pilate asked this question when the Truth was standing right in front of him. And ironically, every Sunday morning, we stand up and say the name of Pontius Pilate. The Truth suffered under Pontius Pilate. The Truth was crucified by the man who represented the world, a man who claimed he would not take a position, who tried to wash his hands of the whole thing. But you cannot be neutral about the truth. And you cannot avoid it. What is Truth? Jesus Christ, who is the same yesterday, today, and forever. Jesus Christ is the truth that is consistent, that does not change, that is distinctive, that is whole, and that is good. And he is the truth that is still under attack. Chesterton says, "Opponents of Christianity will believe anything except Christianity." [31] But the people who attack the Church do

[29] *ILN*, March 16, 1912.
[30] *Handful of Authors*, 127.
[31] *ILN*, January 13, 1906.

not destroy the Church. They only manage to destroy everything else. "Men who begin to fight the Church for the sake of freedom and humanity end by flinging away freedom and humanity if only they may fight the Church."[32] They have tried to take sides with the man who claimed not to be taking sides: Pontius Pilate. They should instead be taking sides with the man that both he and they have condemned.

[32] *Orthodoxy, CW* 1:344.

3

The Limits of Language

Our chief trouble at present is that words and things do not fit each other.

—*Illustrated London News*, December 24, 1910

G. K. Chesterton's vocation was words. He made his living growing words and harvesting them, wrapping them in paper and selling them. And while the man now lies in his grave, and his soul presumably rests in heaven, all of his sparkling ideas and his scintillating arguments and his magnificent explanations live on in the words that he wrote. His verbal fireworks still light up the literary sky. In defending the normal things against the abnormal, in talking sense to a world full of nonsense, in dealing with the use and abuse of logic, he had to deal with the use and abuse of language.

The object of language, says Chesterton, is to be understood.[1] He says that whenever we hear of "things being unutterable and indefinable and impalpable and unnamable and subtly indescribable", then we can be sure that it is a sign of decay.

[1] See *ILN*, January 8, 1927.

Oh, it is perfectly true that there is something in all good things that is beyond all speech or figure of speech. But it is also true that there is in all good things a perpetual desire for expression, for concrete embodiment; and though the attempt to embody it is always inadequate, the attempt is always made. If the idea does not seek to be the word, the chances are that it is an evil idea. If the word is not made flesh it is a bad word.[2]

The foundation of all education is the language in which that education is conveyed, which is why Chesterton argues that if a student has only one thing to learn, he had better learn his language.[3] It is fundamental. The proof of how fundamental it is can be seen in what happens when we do not learn our language. Chesterton says that some of the most enormous and idiotic developments of our modern thought and speech arise simply from not knowing the parts of speech and principles of language.[4] A verb is not a noun. A noun governs a verb. An adjective qualifies a noun; it does not contradict it. If we say, "Give me an undogmatic religion", it is as if we were to say, "Give me an apple pie with no apples in it." In the same way, says Chesterton, the answer to most modern sophistries and other stupidities can be found in a basic book of grammar.

In modern discourse, language is in constant danger of being politicized: words are degraded, and meanings are twisted so that the truth can be avoided, concealed, or ignored. Chesterton says, "It is difficult to believe that people who are obviously careless about language can really be very careful about anything else." [5]

[2] *A Miscellany of Men* (Norfolk, Va.: IHS Press, 2004), 98.
[3] See *The Defendant* (New York: Dodd, Mead, 1904), 130.
[4] See *ILN*, October 16, 1909.
[5] *ILN*, April 4, 1908.

It is assumed that language is a thing which exists for practical purposes. This is clearly untrue: for practical purposes we might very well be content with pointing. Even for purposes of written communication a much simpler and plainer system of symbols might easily be adopted. But language, in its written form, especially exists for the purpose of suggesting shades of thought and starting trains of association. For this entirely poetic and emotional purpose all language exists. For this purpose every word is important. For this purpose every letter in every word is important. The letters are important because they make up the recognisable colour and quantity of the word. It is not an accident that the very word "literature" has a meaning which connects it with the alphabet. It is not an accident that when we speak of a literary man we call him a man of letters.[6]

G. K. Chesterton is truly a man of letters. Truly. He uses his gift for the English language to tell the truth. The right use of language, the whole purpose of talking or writing, is to tell the truth. The wrong use of language is to tell a lie.

Chesterton says that the only thing that can be exaggerated is the truth. "Nothing else can stand the strain."[7] The modern decadent philosophers do not exaggerate; they distort. Or worse, they destroy, or, as they now put it, they deconstruct.

The modern approach to an ancient text, or any text for that matter, is to deconstruct it, to take it apart until there is nothing left of it, to take what it says and make it say less and less until it says nothing at all. We are left with a lot of broken pieces that no longer fit together, words that have been cut off from their meanings. This is the state of modern thinking. It is nothing but fragments—broken, disconnected thoughts.

[6] *ILN*, September 22, 1906.
[7] *Charles Dickens*, *CW* 15:145.

The scientific approach to language will only get as far as the scientific approach to anything else. As soon as we try to observe and measure and analyze anything human, it is the very "human factor" that prevents any neat conclusions. The deconstructionist who attempts to dissect a text the way a pathologist dissects a cadaver does not shed any light on the meaning of life. Chesterton anticipates the basic fallacies of the deconstructionist philosophy.

Every religion and every philosophy must, of course, be based on the assumption of the authority or the accuracy of something. But it may well be questioned whether it is not saner and more satisfactory to ground our faith on the infallibility of the Pope, or even the infallibility of the Book of Mormon, than on this astounding modern dogma of the infallibility of human speech. Every time one man says to another, "Tell us plainly what you mean!" he is assuming the infallibility of language; that is to say, he is assuming that there is a perfect scheme of verbal expression for all the internal moods and meanings of men. Whenever a man says to another, "Prove your case; defend your faith," he is assuming the infallibility of language: that is to say, he is assuming that a man has a word for every reality in earth, or heaven, or hell. He knows that there are in the soul tints more bewildering, more numberless, and more nameless than the colours of an autumn forest; he knows that there are in the world strange and terrible crimes that have never been condemned and virtues that have never been christened. Yet he seriously believes that these things can every one of them, in all their tones and semi-tones, be accurately represented by an arbitrary system of grunts and squeals. He believes that an ordinary civilized stockbroker can really produce out of his own inside noises which denote all the mysteries of memory and all the agonies of desire. Whenever, on the other hand, a man rebels faintly or vaguely against this way of speaking, whenever a man says that he cannot explain what he means, and that he hates argument, that his enemy is misrepresenting him, but he cannot explain how; that man is a true sage, and has seen into the heart of the real nature of language. Whenever a man refuses to be caught by some dilemma about reason and passion, or about reason and faith, or about fate and free-will, he has seen the truth. For the truth is that language is not a scientific thing at all, but wholly an artistic thing, a thing invented by hunters, and killers, and such artists long before science was dreamed of. The truth is simply *that*—that the tongue is not a reliable instrument, like a stopwatch or a camera. The tongue is most truly an unruly member, as the wise saint has called it, a thing poetic and dangerous, like music or fire.[8]

We are always trying to find ways to get at the truth. That is what we expect philosophy to do for us. "All real philosophy", says Chesterton, "is apocalyptic."[9] It is a revelation. It unveils the truth. We all want to know more than what language tells us. We want to see the big picture, but we also want to know how every little picture fits into the big picture. We want to see how everything fits together. It does not matter how good our philosophy looks on paper; what matters is how it works in the real world. Chesterton puts the modern philosophers to shame in two ways: first, by showing how their philosophies are really of no use (they are not connected to the real world), and secondly, by showing how their philosophies are not connected to real people. Philosophy is for everyone. It is not supposed to be something specialized and arid and academic. Chesterton says philosophy is one of the only truly democratic things, because it has to tackle everything and

---

[8] *G. F. Watts* (1910), in *G. K. Chesterton on G. F. Watts* (Compton: Watts Gallery, 2008), 31.

[9] *A Handful of Authors* (New York: Sheed and Ward, 1953), 171.

defend itself against all attacks. "There is no detail, from buttons to kangaroos that does not enter into the [happy] confusion of philosophy." [10] And what is true of philosophy is even more true of theology. Chesterton says, "There is no fact of life, from the death of a donkey to the General Post Office, which has not its place to dance and sing in, in the glorious Carnival of theology." [11]

And so, to take all these great ideas and cosmic truths and then deconstruct them and analyze them through the lens of linguistics is, well, stupid. It is stupid because language itself is subject to the same decline that the rest of mankind is subject to. Language is unique to mankind, but like mankind, it is fallen.

Chesterton explains one of the strange and unfortunate results of fallen creatures working with a fallen language: "We have grown used to a habit of calling things by the wrong names and supporting them by the wrong arguments; and even doing the right thing for the wrong cause." [12]

And if getting our own language to work for us is not hard enough, the problem is compounded when it comes to translation, getting one language to work in another language. Chesterton says, "A good translator will be the first to agree that no translation is good; or, at any rate, good enough." [13] He is always tempted to say that what has to be translated is always what cannot be translated. And yet the vast differences between two different languages are sometimes not as difficult as the subtle differences within the same language.

[10] G. F. Watts, 47.
[11] Ibid.
[12] The New Jerusalem, CW 20:297–98.
[13] St. Thomas Aquinas, CW 2:509.

> The French and English have different words for the same thing; but Americans and English are in a much worse state of botheration. They have the same word for different things.[14]

> I always know what an Italian writer means, even when I disagree with him. I do not know what the English writers mean, even when I agree with them.[15]

But, as it turns out, all communication is translation. It starts with translating our own thoughts into words and continues with someone else translating our words into something they understand. So also, every definition is a translation. When defining a word, we are forced to use different words from the word we are defining. It really does no good, for instance, to call a spade a spade or to say that boys will be boys. There is not, as Chesterton says, "any kind of logical or philosophical use in merely saying the same word twice over." [16]

Every definition hangs on the word "is". We are not saying that one thing is something else. We are trying to explain what *that* something *is*. But we have to explain it in terms of something else. We are trying to understand a word using other words. Knowing nine hundred words, says Chesterton, is not as important as knowing what some of them mean.[17] This is why we need definitions.

There is another great man of letters with whom G. K. Chesterton has often been compared: Dr. Samuel Johnson. Dr. Johnson was a great wit, a great arguer, and he wrote about everything. One of the most amazing things he wrote was a dictionary of the English language. G. K. Chesterton

---

[14] *ILN*, May 18, 1912.
[15] *ILN*, June 7, 1924.
[16] *Appreciations and Criticisms of the Works of Charles Dickens*, *CW* 15:323.
[17] See *Irish Impressions*, *CW* 20:105.

also wrote about everything and certainly could have written a dictionary. He often emphasizes a word by making its meaning wonderfully clear. Here is a sample from the dictionary that Chesterton never wrote, just a few selections from the letter "A":[18]

absent-mindedness: present-mindedness on something else.[19]

actor: a bundle of masks.[20]

adventure: an inconvenience rightly considered.[21]

advertisement: rich people asking for more money.[22]

agnostic: one whose dogma is that there is no dogma.[23]

anger: knowing what you don't want more than what you do.[24]

architecture: the alphabet of giants.[25]

art: the signature of man.[26]

abortion: the mutilation of womanhood and the massacre of men unborn.[27]

---

[18] For more "Chesternitions" see *The Universe According to G. K. Chesterton: A Dictionary of the Mad, Mundane and Metaphysical*, edited by Dale Ahlquist (Mineola, N.Y.: Dover Publications, 2011).

[19] Maisie Ward, *Return to Chesterton* (New York: Sheed and Ward, 1952), 76.

[20] "The Paradise of Thieves", in *The Wisdom of Father Brown*, *CW* 12:270.

[21] *All Things Considered* (New York: Sheed and Ward, 1956), 27.

[22] *The New Jerusalem*, *CW* 20:246.

[23] *Handful of Authors*, 138.

[24] *Century Magazine*, November 1912.

[25] *ILN*, July 19, 1924.

[26] *The Everlasting Man*, *CW* 2:166.

[27] *Eugenics and Other Evils*, *CW* 4:387.

The modern world avoids definitions because it avoids
dogmas. It wants vagueness because it is easy to hide in
the fog. Chesterton says that definitions are very dreadful
things: "[T]hey do the two things that most men, especially
comfortable men, cannot endure. They fight; and they fight
fair." [28]

Those modern thinkers who do not define their terms
do not fight fair. Moreover, they degrade the meanings of
the words we are accustomed to using. And yet, they are
offended when their own position is actually exposed. Chesterton wryly observes: "A modern thinker not only will
not state his own opinion in clear, straightforward English,
but he is hideously affronted if you do it for him." [29]

Chesterton says that words are "perpetually falling below
themselves".[30] The word "culture", for instance, used to
refer to little things that were cared for and were growing
and were full of life, as in "agriculture". Now it means
something large that is itself in the state of decay. "Property" used to mean what was proper to a man. "Ignorant"
used to mean something willful. It was tied to the word
"ignore", an ignorant person being someone *choosing* to
ignore the truth. In other words, sin makes you stupid. And
a society that no longer knows the meaning of "honor" no
longer knows the meaning of "disgrace".

Language falls as we fall. But it rises as we rise.

All prose wants to be poetry, in spite of the fact that
poetry has decayed into prose. Still, every word has the sense
of being an incantation, a magic word. Language is a divine
gift that sets us apart from the other creatures. Like every
other divine gift, it works best when we give it back to
God. We are challenged to build something beautiful with

[28] *Utopia of Usurers*, *CW* 5:422.
[29] *ILN*, August 14, 1909.
[30] *ILN*, May 21, 1927.

these bricks called words. We are trying to write a love letter to God.

When it comes to definitions, how can we possibly define God? We get no help by saying merely that God is God. That is the kind of tautology that the Muslims engage in. No, we say God is our Father. We say the Lord is my Shepherd. We say God is a rock in a weary land, our strength, our refuge, our hope. We say that Jesus Christ is God— Christ who is a lamb, a lion, a fire, a fountain, a physician, a king, a servant.

When Moses asked God what his name is, God replied, "I AM." God *is* is.

And yet, says Chesterton, God is too *actual* to be defined.[31] That, of course, will not stop us from trying to get our words around him. It is part of the task of literature to express the inexpressible.

> A man's soul is as full of voices as a forest; there are ten thousand tongues there like all the tongues of the trees: fancies, follies, memories, madnesses, mysterious fears, and more mysterious hopes. All sanity in life consists in coming to the conclusion that some of those voices have authority and others do not. You may have an impulse to fight your enemy or an impulse to run away from him; a reason to serve your country or a reason to betray it; a good idea for making sweets or a better idea for poisoning them. The only test I know by which to judge one argument or inspiration from another is ultimately this: that all the noble necessities of man talk the language of eternity. When man is doing the three or four things that he was sent on this earth to do, then he speaks like one who shall live for ever. . . . There are in life certain immortal moments, moments that have authority.[32]

[31] See *Charles Dickens, CW* 15:39.
[32] *ILN*, July 2, 1910.

And so, let us talk the language of eternity. An author writes a book. The Author of Life has written the Book of Life. The author has *authority*. The word "authority" has the word author in it. The author uses words. The Word comes from the Author. In the beginning was the Word. And the Word was with God. And the Word was God.

4

The Problem of Evil

Men who wish to get down to fundamentals perceive
that there is a fundamental problem of evil. Men content to be more superficial are also content with a superficial fuss and bustle of improvement.

—*Illustrated London News*, September 1, 1928

There are two kinds of evil. There is the evil that you do
not cause, and the evil that you do. There is the evil that
happens to you, and there is the evil that you help make
happen. There is the evil that you trip over, and the evil
that you pursue.

There is, however, a connection between the two. The
problem of evil is connected directly to the problem of
sin, even though sin itself has to do with a broken connection. Sin is what separates us from God. The problem
of sin is fundamental, and that is why we should deal with
it right at the beginning of this book. In fact, we should
have dealt with it before now. But no one wants to talk
about sin, so we are going to avoid the topic until the
next chapter. But people want to talk about the problem
of evil, even if they do not want to talk about the problem of sin. This is because we are more focused on the

evil that happens to us rather than on the evil we cause to happen.

The problem of evil has certainly bedeviled the claims of Christianity and the belief in a loving God. That nagging question, How could an all-loving, all-powerful God allow evil? is asked sometimes sincerely, but more often tossed down as a challenge to the believer. It seems that there are only four possible answers to the question:

1. God is not all-loving.
2. God is not all-powerful.
3. Evil is not really evil.
4. Um ... like ... you know ... whatever.

Needless to say, none of these answers is satisfactory.

First of all, if God is not all-loving, well then we are simply in an eternity of trouble, and not even buckets full of fear and trembling are going to do us any good. Secondly, if God is not all-powerful, why bother worshipping him? In fact, why not worship evil, since evil is apparently stronger? Thirdly, if there is no evil, then suffering is an illusion. But if suffering is an illusion, I am going to start smacking people I do not like—starting with the fellow who denies the existence of evil. And finally, if, um, like, you know, whatever (or in other words, if there is no God), well then let us just forget the whole thing. The only way to deal with meaninglessness is not to think about it.

Each of the answers provides problems of its own, some real philosophical and theological dilemmas. We have either a God who is too strong or a God who is too weak, or no evil, or no God. If there is no God, how do we even know there is evil? Where did this sense of evil come from? For that matter, where did our sense of good come from? Why is good so good? Nietzsche, of course, dealt with this conundrum by denying God, good, and evil. This brilliant solution cost him his sanity. He spent the last eleven years of his life in a lunatic asylum, muttering the German equivalent of "Um ... like ... you know ... whatever." His obvious madness, however, has not prevented philosophy departments in universities across America from taking his ideas seriously while ignoring Chesterton.

And it is to Chesterton that we now turn. His approach to the problem is to call on common sense. While there are dark days when we may feel like siding with the pessimists and brighter days when we may feel like siding with the optimists, we all know that neither optimism nor pessimism represents a complete philosophy. The world cannot be explained as completely good or completely evil. However, neither can it be explained as half good and half evil, designed like a chessboard of equal parts black and white. The common sense of the common man rejects any of these explanations of life:

> Something tells him that the ultimate idea of a world is not bad or even neutral; staring at the sky or the grass or the truths of mathematics or even a new-laid egg, he has a vague feeling like the shadow of that saying of the great Christian philosopher, St. Thomas Aquinas, "Every existence, as such, is good." On the other hand, something else tells him that it is unmanly and debased and even diseased to minimise evil to a dot or even a blot. He realises that optimism is morbid. It is, if possible, even more morbid than pessimism. These vague but healthy feelings, if he followed them out, would result in the idea that *evil is in some way an exception but an enormous exception; and ultimately that evil is an invasion or yet more truly a rebellion.* He does not think that everything is right or that everything is wrong, or that everything is equally right and wrong. But he does think that right has a right to be right and therefore a right to be

there; and wrong has no right to be wrong and therefore
no right to be there. It is the prince of the world; but it is
also a usurper.[1]

Evil is an invasion. It is a rebellion. The Christian explanation is the best explanation. God created a good world.
He also created creatures with a free will. Not only was
there a Fall of man, which came with the first sin, there
was a fall before the Fall, when the Angel of Light became
the Prince of Darkness. And according to Christian theology, this Prince of Darkness is also the Prince of this world.
The problem of evil can only be explained by understanding that Satan is a reality.

G. K. Chesterton says that he believed in the existence of
the devil even before he believed in the existence of God.
He went through a very dark period as a young man and
had what were apparently very vivid encounters with demonic
presences. But though he was initially drawn to them, as is
often the case with the glamour of evil, he was ultimately
repelled by them. As he was emerging from this dark time
in his life, he had an encounter that not only jolted him
with the reality of the devil, but probably propelled him into
the arms of God. He describes it as "by far the most terrible
thing that has ever happened to me in my life."

What was it? "It was simply a quiet conversation which
I had with another man."[2]

The other man was a fellow art student of Chesterton's
with whom he studied for a brief time at London's Slade
School of Art in the 1890s. We never learn his name, but
he was very intelligent and could engage in deep conversation with anyone, yet he preferred a certain "drunk and

---

[1] *Everlasting Man, CW* 3:376–77. (Emphasis mine.)
[2] See "The Diabolist", in *Tremendous Trifles* (1909; repr., Mineola, N.Y.:
Dover Publications, 2007), 178–83.

dirty" company. And yet, he also took to Chesterton. One wintry evening, when they were standing outside around a fire, the young man turned and suddenly asked, "Chesterton, why are you becoming orthodox?" [3]

Young Gilbert realized at that moment it was true. He responded that he had come to hate modern doubt because it is dangerous.

"You mean dangerous to morality", replied the other. "I expect you are right. But why do you care about morality?" [4]

Chesterton put his great gift of reason to use. He pointed to the fire. The very sparks in it were enough to deduce Christian morality. He said he once thought that pleasure was like a spark that could come and go, that delight was as free as a fire. But then he realized that appreciation of the red spark is connected to virtue, "an invisible pyramid of virtues". The good things we see are only the result of all the good things that we do not see, good things that have been taught to us and have become living habits. We are taught by our mothers to say "thank you" for a slice of bread, so that we can be thankful for every good thing. We like the red in the red sparks because we have been told about the blood of the martyrs. We like the brightness of the sparks, because we have learned that brightness is a glory. "That flame flowered out of virtues, and it will fade with virtues. Seduce a woman, and that spark will be less bright. Shed blood, and that spark will be less red. Be really bad, and they will be to you like the dull pattern on a wallpaper." [5]

To this amazing analysis, the other responded, "But shall I not find in evil a life of its own? Granted that for every

[3] Ibid.
[4] Ibid.
[5] Ibid.

woman I ruin one of those red sparks will go out: but will not the expanding pleasure of ruin ..." [6]

Chesterton did not wait for him to finish that thought. He realized he was talking to someone who had given himself over to evil. "Do you see that fire?" he interrupted. "If we had a real fighting democracy, some one would burn you in it; like the devil-worshipper that you are."

"Perhaps. Only what you call evil I call good." [7]

As Chesterton walked away, he felt the need to cleanse himself of the other's presence. But then he heard the diabolist's voice again, talking to one of the worst of his cronies, who said, "Come, let's do it tonight. Nobody can possibly know."

And the answer Chesterton heard was, "I tell you I have done everything else. If I do that, I shan't know the difference between right and wrong."

Chesterton rushed away, and as he passed the fire he did not know "whether it was hell or the furious love of God".[8]

The atmosphere that Chesterton describes in this scene, his vivid memory of the encounter and the conversation, and his assessment that it was the most terrifying experience of his life are all very striking. The story is meant, I think, to be shocking. Yet, many of us who read Chesterton's narrative of the "Diabolist" are not shocked by it. And that is precisely our problem. We are not shocked enough by evil in a world where evil has become almost commonplace. Chesterton says don't be proud of the fact that your grandmother is shocked by something that doesn't shock you. It may be that your grandmother is alive and a vital person, and you are a paralytic.[9]

[6] Ibid.
[7] Ibid.
[8] Ibid.
[9] See *ILN*, December 16, 1933.

We have reached the point where, as Chesterton points out, "Men do not differ so much about what things they will call evil; they differ enormously about what evils they will call excusable." [10]

Evil has worn us down. "It is possible to do wrong, not through a sudden impatience, but through a dreadful patience—an awful patience with evil." [11]

While it is important to understand evil as the absence of good, it is crucial to remember that evil is very real. The devil is real. He is not simply what shadow is to light. But though he is real, he cannot make anything. Only God can create. The devil can only damage and degrade and destroy. As Chesterton says, "God is a workman and can make things. The Devil is a gentleman and can only destroy them." [12]

While there really are wicked men, like Jack the Ripper, who apparently take a positive pleasure in wickedness, it is important to note that they are the exception even to the work of the devil. The more general work of the devil is to lure us into a passive evil. While it is a spiritual failing to neglect good, it is also an intellectual failing to neglect reason, because reason is good. G. K. Chesterton is always trying to get us to be good by thinking well. When we accept things that are wrong—for instance, when we accept injustice—the mind becomes accustomed to what is untenable or unfair, and unreasonable. Chesterton says, "He who has got used to unreason is ready for unkindness." [13]

Satan is subtle. He does not want credit for his work when he deceives people into thinking that some particular evil is necessary, or that it is inevitable, or even that evil is good. For instance one of the most evil spirits in

[10] *ILN*, October 23, 1909.
[11] *DN*, November 16, 1907.
[12] "The Face of Brass", *CW* 14:735.
[13] *ILN*, March 7, 1908.

our times, according to Chesterton, is the one that convinces people to fall on some material or mechanical explanation for their behavior.[14] This has certainly been the case when it comes to sexual immorality. We blame our behavior on something biological or psychological or sociological, but never theological. When we give in, even just a little, it is not long before we find ourselves sliding into a deep abyss. Chesterton's Father Brown reminds us that we can maintain a level of good, but we cannot maintain a level of evil. That road keeps going down and down.[15] This is especially true of sexual immorality.

> The exaggeration of sex becomes sexlessness. It becomes something that is much worse than mere anarchy, something that can truly be described as malice; a war, not against the restraints required by virtue but against virtue itself. The old moral theology called it malice; and there will be no future for the modern psychology until it again studies the old moral theology. Sex is the bait and not the hook; but in that last extreme of evil the man likes the hook and not the bait.[16]

In the last extreme, sex is emptied of all its beauty and becomes only perversion. But it all begins when sex is separated from its natural purpose, which is conception. Sex becomes a form of evil when, like the devil, it cannot create anything but can only distort and destroy. Chesterton warns that unless we become the enemy of such an evil, we will become not its slave but its champion.[17] "The one danger is not that we may meet devils, but that we may worship them."[18]

[14] See *George Bernard Shaw*, *CW* 11:440.
[15] See "The Flying Stars", in *The Innocence of Father Brown*, *CW* 12:101.
[16] *ILN*, March 30, 1929.
[17] See *ILN*, April 14, 1917.
[18] *The Crimes of England*, *CW* 5:226.

And so we have to fight evil. And that is what the Catholic Church does. When Jesus began his earthly ministry, he came to do battle. The Gospels portray him as a poet and a prophet, but most frequently as an exorcist. He was casting out demons everywhere. Evil has no right to be here, and it must be cast out. It is an invader.

In light of this, it is not surprising that Chesterton says that this world can be made beautiful again by beholding it as a battlefield:

> When we have defined and isolated the evil thing, the colours come back into everything else. When evil things have become evil, good things really become good. There are some men who are dreary because they do not believe in God; but there are many others who are dreary because they do not believe in the devil.[19]

And so it does no good to argue that evil does not exist or that if evil does exist, it proves that God is not all-powerful or all-loving or is not there. The problem of evil, which has been a classic objection to the Christian faith, is actually evidence *for* the Christian faith. Evil proves that the claims of Christianity are valid. The Church teaches that there is an enemy. In a strange way, evil points to the good, even to the truth, because it is always pointing away from it.

Unfortunately that still does not make the problem of evil go away. But one of the ways evil works is that we sometimes convince ourselves that it *has* gone away. When we deny that there is an evil, that is when evil lies close at hand. It works best undercover. This is why we constantly need to expose it for what it is, to bring it out into the open where we may openly do battle with it. Chesterton

[19] *Charles Dickens, CW* 15:202.

says, "God Himself will not help us to ignore evil, but only to defy and to defeat it. But the finding and fighting of positive evil is the beginning of all fun." [20]

We have been promised final victory in this war against evil. It may seem at times that we are losing all the battles along the way to this final victory. But that should not discourage us. On the contrary, as Chesterton reminds us, finding and fighting evil is the beginning of all fun.

[20] *ILN*, April 14, 1917.

5

The Seven Deadly Sins

> The true reason for hating crime is not that we could
> not commit it, but that we could; a better reason still for
> hating crime is that we have committed it.
>
> —*Daily News*, January 29, 1910

Now here's an unpleasant topic: sin. But we are going
to talk about it anyway. In fact, we are going to talk
about seven unpleasant topics, as in the Seven Deadly
Sins. We will try to balance the badness by also talking
about virtue. However, virtue can also be an unpleasant topic—because of our sins. It is uncomfortable to
talk about right and wrong, especially when we are in the
wrong.

But we really do need to talk about it. We cannot fix a
broken world until we face up to the reality of sin. G. K.
Chesterton says:

> The evils of civilization are mainly due to sin, and should
> be corrected with a sense of sin. Let us leave it to the quiet,
> meek materialists to trace all ills to forces and balances, aver-
> age and percentage. [We] ought to be tracing them where
> they are to be traced, to the seven deadly sins, to the

avarice and pride and sloth, and gluttony of everybody, and especially of ourselves.[1]

The Seven Deadly Sins—pride, avarice, envy, anger, gluttony, lust, and sloth—can be listed separately, but it is difficult to discuss them separately. Though we may personally excel at certain sins, they are still tied together. The sins have a way of sticking together. The virtues also have a way of sticking together. Interestingly enough, the virtues complement one another, while the vices seem to contradict one another. For instance, Saint Thomas Aquinas says that demons are frozen in pride and envy. Now, if you think about it, these are almost opposites. Pride is based on the idea that I am superior to you, and envy is based on the idea that you are superior to me. Which is probably why Saint Thomas also says that the demons are not a happy tribe.

And that is the main point about sin. It makes us unhappy. We sin, of course, thinking it is going to make us happy. Instead, it makes us *un*happy.

Happiness is based on obedience. It is what G. K. Chesterton calls "the Doctrine of Conditional Joy".[2] It is illustrated in every fairy tale. Get home before midnight or the coach will turn into a pumpkin. It is of course the story of mankind's very first sin. The Garden of Eden was a paradise. The man and the woman enjoyed every delight and could continue to do so. They just had to follow one rule. Guess what happened.

Chesterton points out that the whole human race has a tradition of the Fall. Every cult and culture, one older than another, "all lead back to one idea that man held happiness

[1] *DN*, May 8, 1909.
[2] *Orthodoxy*, *CW* 1:258.

on a condition, and is unhappy through breaking that condition." [3]

Sin is not merely a blunder; it is deliberate disobedience. It is an act of the will. That is its shame. Obedience is also deliberate. It is also an act of the will. That is its glory. For Chesterton, one of the most important precepts of the Catholic Church, one that really sets it apart from all the ancient and modern heresies, is free will. It means we cannot blame our sins on anybody or anything else except ourselves. Evil is something we choose. It is true that on occasion we encounter evil that we have not chosen, but the question is, how will we respond?

Who better to explain it than a priest? Chesterton's priest, Father Brown.

> Human troubles are mostly of two kinds. There is an accidental kind, that you can't see because they are so close you fall over them as you do over a hassock.[4]

> And there is the other kind of evil, the real kind. And that a man will go to seek however far off it is—down, down, into the lost abyss.[5]

The Seven Deadly Sins are not the mortal sins. They are not actual actions. They are the state that our soul has entered so that we commit acts of sin, including mortal sin. They are called "deadly" for the simple reason that if we pursue any of these sins, they will destroy us.

People do not like to talk about sin. They prefer to talk about morality. Well, they do not like talking about morality either. Nevertheless, the word "morality" seems less harsh

---

[3] "Tagtug and the Tree of Knowledge", *The Coloured Lands* (New York: Sheed and Ward, 1938), 140.

[4] A hassock is an ottoman. What's an ottoman? It is one of those overstuffed footrests in an overstuffed living room—something you trip over.

[5] "The Donnington Affair", *CW* 14:149.

and more open to interpretation than the word "sin". Chesterton is struck by the term "current morality". It certainly sounds better than the "current sin". But then Chesterton wonders what the term "current morality" means. He suggests it means "the morality that is always running away".[6]

Along the same line, he also observes that we do not really have any disputes about what we call evil, only about what evils we call excusable.[7]

This change that Chesterton observes is very dangerous for our souls, for it is a change not in the sins for which sinners are punished, but in the sins for which they are not punished, that is, the sins that are no longer regarded as sins at all.

> It is in the things taken for granted; the things passed over; even the things forgotten, that the glaring change appears. It is involved in the very words used to whitewash it. People say, "There were blackguards like that a hundred years ago and in every age." The answer is "Yes; there were blackguards like that a hundred years ago. But there were not respectable people like that a hundred years ago. Society did not assume a convention of sin, which only became unconventional when it actually turned into crime. It is not that more people have broken the law; it is that the law is broken; broken in the sense of having broken down."[8]

But just as there are no new sins, there are no former sins that have been upgraded into virtues. Morality has not changed, in spite of our attempts to change it. We try to defy sin, but we only defy God with the same old sins. The

---

[6] *Orthodoxy*, *CW* 1:314.
[7] See *ILN*, October 23, 1909.
[8] *G. K.'s Weekly*, April 4, 1925.

main reason we no longer recognize sin is that we no longer recognize virtue. Why is that? Chesterton has the answer: "The terrible danger at the heart of our Society is that the tests are giving way. We are altering, not the evils, but the standard of good which is the only standard by which any evil can be detected and defined."[9]

There is one institution in the world that still calls sin "sin". It is the Catholic Church, which is, ironically, made up entirely of sinners. The Church has the unenviable task of explaining that there are things that the world holds up as rights that are actually wrongs. The Church will not compromise with sin. In other words, it will not excuse sin. But it will forgive sin. Not compromising with sin is an act of mercy, because only admitting that sin is sin is what will make us better. It is called confession.

> There are many critics who claim that it is morbid to confess your sins. But the morbid thing is *not* to confess them. The morbid thing is to conceal your sins and let them eat away at your soul, which is exactly the state of most people in today's highly civilized communities.[10]

> It sometimes does people good to punish them. It often, probably more often, does them good to pardon them. It more often does them good to understand them, and so absolve them with a serious spiritual authority.[11]

The new ways of dealing with sin do not work—only the old way.

Chesterton's friend and fellow mystery writer Dorothy L. Sayers once recounted that someone said to her, "I

[9] *ILN*, March 25, 1911.
[10] *DN*, January 8, 1908.
[11] *ILN*, April 4, 1914.

did not know there were seven deadly sins. Please tell me the names of the other six." [12]

We can tell you what the worst of the Seven Deadly Sins is. It is pride. If there were seven chapters in this book devoted to the Seven Deadly Sins, six of the chapters would have to be about pride.

All of the sins are a form of self-indulgence. But pride is the chief sin. And humility is the chief virtue. God's greatest demonstration of his love was an act of humility, becoming a man and sacrificing himself, dying a horrible death to save his own creation. Likewise, all human love, which is but a dim reflection of divine love, is an act of humility. Love is the emptying of self, directing our attention, our affection, our concern, our effort, our will, to God and our neighbor, who is made in the image of God (and is sometimes as mysterious as God).

Before even considering the theological issues, Chesterton illustrates the sin of pride in artistic or even mathematical terms. "The evil of pride consists in being out of proportion to the universe." [13]

But it is in theological terms that pride must be discussed. And here, according to Chesterton, pride is the ultimate human evil. It is the last insult to God. It is the sin that denies sin. It means failing in self-criticism, and abounding in self-praise. And Chesterton says that if he had only one sermon to preach, it would be a sermon against pride.

> The more I see of existence ... the more I am convinced
> of the reality of the old religious thesis; that all evil began
> with some attempt at superiority.... Pride is a poisoning

---

[12] Dorothy L. Sayers, *The Whimsical Christian* (New York: Collier Books, 1987), 157.

[13] *Tremendous Trifles* (1909; repr., Mineola, N.Y.: Dover Publications, 2007), 4.

so very poisonous that it not only poisons the virtues; it even poisons the other vices.... The wickedest work in this world is symbolized not by a wine glass but by a looking-glass; and it is not done in public houses, but in the most private of all private houses; which is a house of mirrors.... Pride consists in a man making his personality the only test, instead of making the truth the test....

Is it not true that pride gives to every other vice an extra touch of the intolerable? ... I think the instinct of mankind against pride, as the ultimate human evil, can be proved from the most prosaic details.... Nobody ever hated a miser. Fundamentally, everybody pitied him.... The miser [never] minded looking like a fool. Therefore men have always joked about the miser.... The real beggar was funny: the false beggar was even funnier.... The usurers and princes of avarice were never [hated] until there had been added to them that dynamite detail which we call pride.

But our modern rich have abandoned the wise precautions of the misers of old. The misers hid their wealth. Today's millionaires display it.... The miser is ashamed of being a miser; but our modern millionaire is not ashamed of being a millionaire.... He believes that since he admires himself all other men will admire him as well.

I believe the sin of pride is at the root of all other sins. Gluttony is a great fault; but we do not necessarily dislike a glutton. We only dislike the glutton when he becomes the *gourmet*—that is, we only dislike him when he not only wants the best for himself, but when he knows what is best for other people. It is the poison of pride that has made the difference. Sloth is a great fault: but we do not necessarily dislike the sluggard. We only dislike the sluggard when he becomes the aesthete—the man who need not do anything, but need only "exist beautifully." It is the poison of pride that has made the difference.[14]

[14] *The Common Man* (New York: Sheed and Ward, 1950), 246–55.

And Chesterton adds that if he had only one sermon to preach, he is confident that he would not be asked to preach another.

The next deadly sin? Avarice, greed: the idea that more money, more wealth, more of everything is always better. "There are many definite methods, honest and dishonest, which make people rich; the only instinct I know of that drives such methods is that instinct which theological Christianity crudely describes as 'the sin of avarice.' " [15]

Avarice is the sin that drives unbridled capitalism. "It is not mere business", says Chesterton. "It is mysticism; the horrible mysticism of money." [16] But it is also the great temptation of the politician. It can subject him to blackmail or even treason. In other words, it can lead not only to his own ruin but to the ruin of the nation or state he serves. A politician's blunders may not be his fault, but scandals are his fault.

While avarice feeds the flame of big industry and big industrialists, as well as the big politicians who would do their bidding, it also feeds smaller flames to the ruin of smaller men. All those get-rich-quick schemes and books on success are nothing more than packaged and printed avarice. These books, says Chesterton, "do not teach people to be successful, but they do teach people to be snobbish; they ... spread a sort of evil poetry of worldliness. The Puritans are always denouncing books that inflame lust; what shall we say of books that inflame the viler passions of avarice and pride?" [17]

The first way to get rid of avarice, as of any sin, is to repent. But Chesterton says, "We have lost the idea of repentance; especially in public things; that is why we cannot

---

[15] *ILN*, November 2, 1907.
[16] Ibid.
[17] Ibid.

really get rid of our great national abuses", in both our economic and political tyrannies.[18]

Avarice was one sin that did not tempt G. K. Chesterton: "I am not interested in wealth beyond the dreams of avarice— since I know that avarice has no dreams, but only insomnia." [19]

The sleeplessness of the rich is an old problem. We see it revealed in the Old Testament book of Ecclesiastes: "Sweet is the sleep of a laborer, whether he eats little or much; but the surfeit of the rich will not let him sleep." [20]

This brings us to the next deadly sin, a sin that can also lead to sleepless nights: envy. Chesterton mostly refers to envy in a paradoxical sense. He says he envies the people caught in the London flood because they will know what it is like to live in Venice. He envies people stranded on a desert island because they will know what it is like to have peace and quiet.

Even more paradoxically, he points out the strange lack of envy in the modern world, saying that there is something wrong in a society when ordinary people are out of touch with ordinary sins.

> Just as it is a bad economic sign in the State that masses of our fellow-citizens are too poor to be taxed, so it is a bad ethical sign in the State that masses of our neighbours have become too dulled to be envied. That sort of superiority to envy is not enviable.[21]

> There is something wrong with a man if he does not want to break the ten commandments.[22]

You read that right. There is something wrong with a man if he does not want to break the Ten Commandments.

[18] *A Miscellany of Men* (Norfolk, Va.: IHS Press, 2004), 145.
[19] Ibid., 39.
[20] Ecclesiastes 5:12.
[21] *ILN*, April 11, 1925.
[22] Ibid.

If the conditions of our society have dulled our free will, we have lost our human dignity. Sin is supposed to be a temptation. We could even say sin is supposed to be easy. It usually is. The difficult thing is to be good, to be virtuous, to be obedient. It is a choice, a difficult choice to make: the choice not to sin. If we have become so numbed, so passive, as to not be tempted, we are, well, probably guilty of the sin of sloth. But we will talk about sloth later—if we feel like it.

Back to envy. The envious man is not content to live his own life, but wants to live everyone else's life. He is not content to be himself, but wants to be everyone else.

Most of advertising is designed on directly appealing to the sin of envy. Every available flat surface is plastered with an image of somebody who has something that you do not have. And you are made to feel that you will not be happy unless you have it too. And what economists call "competition" in commerce and industry is always in danger of being driven by envy.

While all of the virtues counter all of the vices, there are two virtues that especially counter the sin of envy: kindness and contentment. One has to do with our relationship with our neighbor, and the other with our relationship with God. In other words, obeying the great commandments of loving God and loving our neighbor is what makes us fulfilled. Happiness is a choice. We can choose to be happy, rather than imagining ourselves unhappy because we do not have something that someone else has, or being unhappy simply because someone else is happy. If we rejoice with those who rejoice, we are rejoicing. We are not envying. If we are busy being kind to our neighbor, we are less driven to envy him. And if we are content with what God has given us, we are less likely to envy our neighbor. Both virtues are based on thankfulness. Chesterton says thanks is the highest form of thought.[23] He tells us to be pleased, "positively pleased", with what we have.

> Being content with bread and cheese ought not to mean not caring what you eat. It ought to mean caring for bread and cheese; handling and enjoying the cubic content of the bread and cheese and adding it to your own.[24]

> True contentment is ... the power of getting out of a situation all that there is in it.[25]

> The voices of the saints and sages, recommending contentment, should sound unceasingly, like the sea.[26]

Next up is anger. It seems that whenever we talk about our own anger, we try to defend it. We refer to justifiable anger, to righteous indignation. But the need for those adjectives indicates that anger is often not justifiable and not righteous. Righteous indignation is a reaction to an injustice. But even the connection between anger and justice is dangerous. Every passion, even the passion for justice, must be controlled by reason. Saint James tells us to "be quick to hear, slow to speak, [and] slow to anger, for the anger of man does not work the righteousness of God." [27] The other word for "righteousness" is "justice". So, the uncontrolled anger of man does not work the *justice* of God. Saint Paul reminds us of God's words: "Vengeance is mine, I will repay, says the Lord." [28] And Saint James further reminds us, "[M]ercy triumphs over judgment." [29]

---

[23] See *A Short History of England, CW* 20:463.
[24] *DN*, June 10, 1911.
[25] Ibid.
[26] *The Apostle and the Wild Ducks* (London: Paul Elek, 1975), 169.
[27] James 1:19–20.
[28] Romans 12:19.
[29] James 2:13.

We get angry at the weeds, but if we are not careful, in our rage, we will end up tearing up the food and the flowers as well. God has given us reason to govern our behavior, and only with the exercise of reason are we free, because only then can we control our actions. It is when we abandon reason that our passion-driven actions control us. Think of how awkward it is to be around someone who has "flown off the handle", or who is in a "frightful" rage. Anger is a deadly sin because it is a loss of control, and it is often a very deadly loss of control—as in second-degree murder.

And think of the term "all the rage". It refers to a kind of popular madness that we call fashion, when an idea sweeps up the crowd, rather than the crowd sweeping up the idea. Most things that are all the rage pass away very quickly, thank God, but not, unfortunately, without doing damage. And there is often a real connection between anger and fashion. We are seduced by the new because we are angry at the old, upset with the past, resentful of tradition. Reformers can be very angry people.

We may unleash our anger at something in particular, like a drawer that won't open. Chesterton says when a drawer is jammed, we often refer to it with a word that rhymes with jammed.[30] But if we think about it, it's not really the drawer's fault that it does not open. Shall we really give the drawer that much power over us that we should act like fools because we cannot get it open?

Anger seems to be pointed and yet it is usually unfocused. Think of the anger of feminists. They are riled up with resentment, and utterly joyless. Think of the obscene defiance of militant homosexuals. They claim to be fighting for freedom and dignity. But their behavior is anything but dignified,

---

[30] See the essay "On Running after One's Hat", in *All Things Considered* (New York: Sheed and Ward, 1956), 24.

and their demand for freedom is really the demand to be enslaved by disordered sexual passions (another deadly sin waiting to be discussed). They aim their anger at the Church, whose teachings certainly condemn their behavior, but where does their anger really come from, and where does it really lead them? "Men who begin to fight the Church for the sake of freedom and humanity end by flinging away freedom and humanity if only they may fight the Church." [31]

This is the problem with rage. It leads to bad behavior, but it also leads to bad thinking. We use the word "mad" to mean "angry", but the word "mad" originally meant crazy, as in madness. But there is a connection between rage and madness; there is a connection between anger and lunacy. Both represent a loss of reason, as well as a loss of the virtue of operating within the normal limits of behavior. For Chesterton, most modern philosophy is madness, or leads to madness. [32] But most modern philosophy is also edgy and angry, because it is rebellious, based on the rejection of the Church's teachings, and the divorce of faith and reason.

Chesterton describes the deadly sin of anger as the swelling of negative emotions that makes us lose control—in other words, bad moods. People who leave the Church usually don't flee because they have carefully thought things out and found a superior creed elsewhere. They usually leave because they are in a bad mood. It is a bad mood that makes us neglect our commitments and abandon our creeds. And, as Chesterton says, the whole purpose of a religion with a fixed creed is that it survives our moods. [33]

The next deadly sin is gluttony. Let's start by pointing out that smoking is not a sin. Drinking is not sin. And for

[31] *Orthodoxy, CW* 1:344.
[32] This is the argument made in chapter 2 of *Orthodoxy*, "The Maniac".
[33] See *Lunacy and Letters* (London: Sheed and Ward, 1958), 122.

the record, dancing is not a sin—although if you ever saw me dance, you would understand why it should be prohibited. It is a misunderstanding of the sin of gluttony to condemn a simple pleasure rather than the abuse of that pleasure. But it is more than a misunderstanding; it is an attack on freedom.

> It is a savage trait to talk about material substances instead of about ideas.... The old civilisation talked about the sin of gluttony or excess. We talk about the Problem of Drink—as if drink could be a problem. When people have come to call the problem of human intemperance the Problem of Drink, and to talk about curing it by attacking the drink traffic, they have reached quite a dim stage of barbarism. The thing is an inverted form of fetish worship; it is no sillier to say that a bottle is a god than to say that a bottle is a devil.[34]

It is not drink but drunkenness that is evil. Anything that takes away our free will is evil. If we are slaves of mere appetite, then we are no different from animals. The Church calls for fasting for the simple reason that it gives us a chance to demonstrate that we are spiritual creatures as well as physical creatures, and that we can rule our appetites rather than have our appetites rule us. To deny a simple pleasure is a simple form of sacrifice. To indulge in a simple pleasure until it ceases even to be a pleasure is sin. It is gluttony.

There is a time for feasting, just as there is a time for fasting. We cannot perpetually feast, just as we cannot perpetually fast. Too much pleasure destroys pleasure. Chesterton says that a man should keep sober enough to praise wine. And he gives us a sound rule for drinking, which like other sound rules is a paradox:

[34] *ILN*, August 18, 1906.

Drink because you are happy, but never because you are miserable. Never drink when you are wretched without it, or you will be like the gray-faced gin-drinker in the slum; but drink when you would be happy without it, and you will be like the laughing peasants of Italy. Never drink because you think you need it, for this is rational drinking, and the way to death and hell. But drink because you do not need it, for this is irrational drinking, and the ancient health of the world.[35]

Now, as for overeating, there are some people who assume that G. K. Chesterton was fat because he ate too much, that he was perhaps a glutton. But Chesterton scholars—both of them—disagree about the reasons for Chesterton's great size. The scholar Geir Hasnes contends that he was not really that fat, at least not disproportionately so.[36] Weighing in on this large subject, Chesterton's secretary Dorothy Collins let it be known that she was amazed at how little he ate.[37] We know that he joked about his great size, and we also know that he freely and humbly admitted his faults, but he never said that gluttony was one of them.[38] So he probably wasn't a glutton. Fatness is not a sin. As Chesterton says, "It may be that the thin monks were holy, but I am sure it was the fat monks who were humble."[39] That very Chestertonian monk, Saint Thomas Aquinas, comes to mind.

[35] *Heretics, CW* 1:92.

[36] Geir Hasnes argued this point at the 25th Annual G. K. Chesterton Conference, St. Paul, Minnesota, June 16, 2006. He even said that Chesterton was no fatter than Dale Ahlquist.

[37] Dorothy Collins, "Reflections", in *G. K. Chesterton: A Centenary Appraisal*, ed. John Sullivan (New York: Barnes and Nobles Books, 1974), 160.

[38] Chesterton admitted to the sins of "laziness, yes, and certain kinds of anger" (Maisie Ward, *Return to Chesterton* [New York: Sheed and Ward, 1952], 298).

[39] *ILN*, May 8, 1909.

The next deadly sin: lust. The one you've been waiting for. There is absolutely nothing that I want to say about lust. I will let Chesterton do all the talking:

> About sex especially men are born unbalanced; we might almost say men are born mad. They scarcely reach sanity till they reach sanctity.[46]

> The two first facts which a healthy boy or girl feels about sex are these: first that it is beautiful and then that it is dangerous.... [A]ll people have an absolutely clean instinct in the matter. Mankind declares with one deafening voice: that sex may be ecstatic so long as it is also restricted. It is not necessary that the restriction should be reasonable; it is only necessary that it should restrict. That is the beginning of all purity; and purity is the beginning of all passion. In other words, the creation of conditions for love, or even for flirting, is common-sense.[41]

> All healthy men, ancient and modern, Western and Eastern, hold that there is in sex a fury that we cannot afford to inflame; and that a certain mystery must attach to the instinct if it is to [be] sane. There are people who maintain that they can talk about this topic as coldly and openly as about any other; there are people who maintain that they would walk naked down the street. But these people are not only insane, they are in the most emphatic sense of the word stupid. They do not think; they only point (as children do) and ask "Why?" ... "Why cannot we discuss sex coolly and rationally anywhere?" This is a tired and unintelligent question. It is like asking, "Why does not a man walk on his hands as well as on his feet?" It is silly. If a man walked systematically on his hands, they would not be hands, but feet. And if love or lust were things that we could all discuss without any possible emotion, they would not be love

---

[40] *The Everlasting Man*, CW 2:248.
[41] *ILN*, January 9, 1909.

or lust, they would be something else—some mechanical function or abstract natural duty which may or may not exist in animals or in angels, but which has nothing at all to do with sex.... Sex is not an unconscious or innocent thing, but an intense and powerful thing, a special and violent emotional stimulation that is at once spiritual and physical. A man who asks us to have no emotions in sex is asking us to have no emotions about emotion.... It may be said of him, in the strict meaning of the words, that he does not know what he is talking about.... There is such a thing as a system of deliberate erotic stimulants. It is called pornography. This is not a thing to be argued about with one's intellect, but to be stamped on with one's heel. If a man tries to excite a sex instinct which is too strong already, he *must* be a scoundrel.[42]

Sex is not a thing like eating and sleeping. There is something dangerous and disproportionate in its place in human nature, for whatever reason; and it does really need a special purification and dedication.... If sex is treated merely as one innocent natural thing among others, what happens is that every other innocent natural thing becomes soaked and sodden with sex.[43]

The moment sex ceases to be a servant it becomes a tyrant.[44]

Enough of that. We have only one deadly sin left: sloth. Interestingly enough, other than pride, the deadliest of the deadly sins, Chesterton wrote more about sloth than about any of the others, perhaps because it was, by his own admission, his own greatest weakness—which is hard to imagine if you consider how much he wrote. In fact, he complains, "For my own part, I never can get enough Nothing to do.

[42] *Common Man*, 125–26.
[43] *St. Francis of Assisi*, *CW* 2:39.
[44] Ibid.

I feel as if I had never had leisure to unpack a tenth part of the luggage of my life and thoughts." [45]

Sloth is not just laziness. It is neglect of duty. If the other deadly sins involve actively doing the wrong thing, sloth is the passive sin of failing to do the right thing.

> A man may be naturally slothful and rather irresponsible; he may neglect many duties through carelessness, and his friends may still understand him, so long as it is really a careless carelessness. But it is work of the devil when a man engages in careful carelessness. It is the work of the devil when a man becomes a deliberate and self-conscious Bohemian ... despising better men than himself, men who work that he may waste. [46]

The classification of the deadly sins came about in the Middle Ages. Chesterton argues that this was the period in our civilization when common sense was at its peak. Common sense is about balance and proportion, maintaining everything in its proper place. And so Chesterton says that what the medievals meant, by dividing and labeling the Seven Deadly Sins, was that a man might fall into one of these sins even when fleeing too far from another. For instance, "A man who neglects his business may fall into sloth; a man who pursues his business may fall into avarice." [47] But after the Renaissance, that balance was lost. Some vices were unleashed on the excuse that others might be exterminated. And so, Chesterton concludes, "The Pagans went in for unlimited lust and the Puritans for unlimited avarice; on the excuse that at least neither of them was being guilty of sloth." [48]

[45] *Autobiography*, *CW* 16:202.
[46] *Common Man*, 249.
[47] *Chaucer*, *CW* 18:330.
[48] Ibid.

One of the ironies about the sin of sloth in the modern world is that it is customary to associate dirt with evil because it is considered evidence of sloth, but as Chesterton points out, "the classes that wash most are those that work least." [49] He also points out that though sloth is the vice most condemned in the modern business world, it is the sin most indulged in, in the modern brain. Our brains show real signs of sluggishness and inactivity. Thinking is hard work, and generally we avoid it.

> It is customary to complain of the bustle and strenuousness of our epoch. But in truth the chief mark of our time is a profound laziness and fatigue, and, ironically, the real laziness is the cause of our apparent bustle. The streets are noisy with taxicabs and motorcars; but this is not due to human activity but to human repose. There would be less bustle if there were more activity, if people were simply walking about. Our world would be more silent if it were more strenuous. And what is true of the apparent physical bustle is true also of the apparent bustle of the intellect. Most of the machinery of modern language is labour-saving machinery. The problem is that it saves mental labour very much more than it ought. Scientific phrases are used like scientific wheels and piston-rods to make swifter and smoother yet the path of the comfortable. Long words go rattling by us like long railway trains. But I fear they are carrying thousands who are too tired or too indolent to walk and think for themselves. It is a good exercise to try ... to express any opinion one holds in words of one syllable. [50]

Although money is the motive for creating labor-saving devices, laziness is the motive for buying such devices. Chesterton says that we are dreaming of a "machine that will

---

[49] *What's Wrong with the World*, CW 4:223.
[50] *Orthodoxy*, CW 1:329.

render needless the labour of thinking."[51] We already use catchwords as substitutes for thinking, thereby limiting our vocabulary along with the use of our brains. In popular science we use the names Darwin and Einstein as if we knew all that is meant by those names. But we don't know. We are not ready to pick up the sharp tools of reason and put them to work to test the modern philosophies. And the only alternative to logic, says Chesterton, is laziness.[52]

We talked about sloth being a passive sin. Passiveness can lead to what Chesterton calls "the unpardonable sin [of] being bored".[53] Boredom, he says, is "the next condition to death ... a decay of vitality."[54] Boredom also represents the loss of imagination, which is one of God's greatest gifts. And the passiveness of boredom, of failing to do the right thing, can lead to despair, a morbid helplessness to do the right thing.

Despair may lead us to sin. Defiance may lead us to sin. But sin never solves any problem. Sin never sets anyone free. Only the truth can set us free. Chesterton found the truth when he discovered the Christian faith. He says that the more he considered Christianity, the more he "found that while it had established a rule and order, the chief aim of that order was to give room for good things to run wild."[55] And he eventually came to embrace the Catholic Church, which he found to be the greatest defender of reason and liberty in the modern world. None of the modern philosophies proved to be as good. And almost all of the modern philosophies tried in some way to do away with sin.

[51] *ILN*, December 3, 1927.
[52] See *ILN*, August 2, 1919.
[53] *Lunacy and Letters*, 56.
[54] Ibid., 57.
[55] *Orthodoxy*, *CW* 1:300.

Every good thing can be perverted. Every bad thing can be whitewashed. The modern world has tried to take the Seven Deadly Sins and transform them into virtues, to exalt them and give them a new name. We have exalted lust by calling it "free love" or "gay rights". We have exalted avarice by calling it "opportunism". We have exalted envy by calling it "the drive to succeed". We have exalted anger by calling it "assertiveness". We have exalted sloth by calling it "tolerance". And we have exalted pride by calling it "self-esteem". As Chesterton says, "A new philosophy generally means the praise of some old vice." [56]

There is only one proper way to deal with sin, and that is to admit that it is sin. It is good to call sin what it is, but that means not only denouncing it but also confessing it. As G. K. Chesterton reminds us, "The modern weakness is that denunciation of sin is not balanced by confession of sin." [57]

---

[56] *ILN*, January 6, 1906.
[57] *DN*, January 29, 1910.

6

The Universe and Other Little Things

We may scale the heavens and find new stars innumerable, but there is still the new star we have not found—
that one on which we were born.

—"A Defence of Planets", *The Defendant*

What do we see when we look into the eyes of a baby that is three months old? G. K. Chesterton says we see "astonishment at the universe". It is perfectly normal and right to be astonished at the universe, though often we neglect the universe, and even forget about it. Sometimes we have to be startled into remembering the universe, in which case we are once again astonished at it. "Astonishment at the universe", says Chesterton, "is not mysticism but a transcendental common sense." [1]

But why are we astonished at the universe? Not simply because it is big. That alone is not a good enough reason. If something needs size in order to be significant, it means that it really is not significant. The largeness of the universe does not mean anything because the universe is unique. There are no other universes to compare it to. It may seem large to *us*, but then so does an elephant. But the reason we like

[1] *The Defendant* (New York: Dodd, Mead, 1904), 112.

elephants is, not because they are large, but because they are cute. They have that irresistible elephantine appeal. They are slow and thoughtful and can do interesting things with their noses.

Chesterton says that he likes the universe, not because it is vast, but because it is cozy. It is just the right size. He finds that he is rather fond of the universe. When we are fond of something, we often address it in the diminutive. And there is a certain charm and sweetness and good humor in naming an elephant Tiny. And there is no reason why we cannot address this dear thing, the universe, in the diminutive. Chesterton says he has often done just that, and the universe never seemed to mind.[2]

This paradoxical view of the universe has implications on several levels.

> Science boasts of the distance of its stars; of the terrific remoteness of the things of which it has to speak. But poetry and religion always insist upon the proximity, the almost menacing closeness of the things with which they are concerned."[3]

I do believe there is some truth in that principle, concerning the material manifestation of good things; that it is material, but it is limited. When material things grow too large, men lose the sense that they are even material, and they take on the darker character of abstractions. Thus the measurement of the material universe, by modern science, by mere size, ceases to be real, and men do not believe that moons so far away are moons at all. So money may be merely mud, but mountains of money are something much worse than mud and far less than mountains. They become merely

[2] See *Orthodoxy*, *CW* 1:266.
[3] *Tremendous Trifles* (1909; repr., Mineola, N.Y.: Dover Publications, 2007), 184–85.

noughts in a ledger; that is the endless addition of nothing to nothing.[4]

If we are going to look at the universe as small and precious, how else can we possibly view that sparkling little jewel in the universe known as the earth? It is the most interesting star in the sky and the most undiscovered. By viewing the earth as small and precious, and also as menacingly close, we can begin to form the proper attitude toward it, which is an issue of great concern to many people today, while to others, the issue is simply a nuisance.

Chesterton says, "The way to love anything is to realize that it might be lost."[5] That is how we should love this little thing, the earth. There is a term to describe loving what is small, reverence for what is weak, caring about "the things that cling in corners". The term is "chivalry". A romantic idea. But Chesterton says, "There never was a scheme nearer to the deepest reality of life than that of the old romance of chivalry."[6]

Man is sent forth by an authority that is good, like King Arthur or a fairy godmother, into a world that is wonderful, but contains dangers and temptations, like dragons and wizards; ... he is sent upon a quest or trial; that is, ... he is judged by the same authority that sent him forth. That is the story at the heart of all healthy life and literature; and it is quite true that people who are healthy can sometimes act on it without arguing it out. But if they *do* argue it out, they will find it implies certain dogmas; as that there is a design, that it is a benevolent design, but that it does allow of free will, and makes the good a matter of choice. Those who thought they could hold that healthy romance forever,

---

[4] *The Resurrection of Rome*, *CW* 21:445–46.
[5] *Tremendous Trifles*, 38.
[6] *ILN*, October 3, 1925.

merely by being healthy and without holding any of the dogmas that justify it, are more and more finding out their mistake. Hence, when they are asked to state what they really do believe about life, they become "desperately vague." And they have now reached the point where it is not only more and more difficult to state a creed, but even more and more difficult to tell a story.[7]

While we are on this subject of appreciating things in their smallness, rescuing wonderful things from terrible things, I would like to point out that the real solution to our economic crisis—as well as to any potential environmental crisis—lies in Chesterton's ideas about Distributism. If that small thing, the traditional family, were recognized as the basic unit of society, something that must be kept together so that the society can be kept together, and if more laborers became owners so that we had more small, locally owned businesses, we could reduce or eliminate our dependence on largeness, on big government and big business, on a global economy with its huge demands on our resources, on huge transportation networks that move everything around so that everything ends up looking the same. Chesterton says that Rousseau's line that "[m]an is born free but everywhere is in chains" is a reference to chain stores.[8] I mention all this right here because it is certainly relevant, but also because you are probably going to skip chapter 12, which is about economics, just like you skipped the last chapter, which was about sin.

Whether it is art or commerce or government or nature, there is more inspiration in the small and the local than in the large and remote.

When we have understood this fact we shall have understood something of the reason why the world has always

[7] Ibid.
[8] *ILN*, April 11, 1936.

been first inspired by small nationalities. The vast Greek
philosophy could fit easier into the small city of Athens
than into the immense Empire of Persia. In the narrow streets
of Florence Dante felt that there was room for Purgatory
and Heaven and Hell. He would have been stifled by the
British Empire. Great empires are necessarily prosaic; for it
is beyond human power to act a great poem upon so great
a scale. You can only represent very big ideas in very small
spaces.[9]

Purgatory. How did that come up all of the sudden? Well,
if we all thought more about purgatory, we could solve our
environmental problems. If we thought more about prepar-
ing to meet God face-to-face, we would be more thoughtful
about how we cared for his creation. If we thought more
about heaven, we would take better care of the earth—but
not for the earth's sake. The reason for taking care of the
earth is that we are obeying a commandment when we do so,
and we are breaking a commandment when we fail to do so.
The commandment is the one about loving our neighbor.
Taking care of the earth is a way of loving our neighbor. We
love our neighbor by not polluting the stream. We love our
neighbor by not wasting resources that our neighbor might
need, especially our neighbor who has not been born yet.

What is the proper attitude toward nature? This is where
Chesterton really helps us with a very simple and striking
perspective: "Nature is not our Mother. Nature is our sister", because "we both have the same father." We can be
proud of her beauty, we can laugh at her and love her, "but
she has no authority over us." [10]

This is a healthier perspective than that of those who,
whether they are willing to admit it or not, worship the

[9] *Tremendous Trifles*, 122.
[10] *Orthodoxy*, CW 1:317.

earth itself, who speak of Nature as a knowing force, who ascribe every occurrence in the plant or animal kingdom as somehow an acting out of Nature's own purpose. Chesterton exposes the assumptions that are at work when someone starts referring to Nature with a little too much reverence: "To talk of the purpose of Nature is to make a vain attempt to avoid being anthropomorphic, merely by being feminist. It is believing in a goddess because you are too sceptical to believe in a god." [11] And this is why he maintains that "what some of us call Nature, the wiser of us call Creation." [12] Nature cannot have a purpose; only creation can have a purpose.

If the earth is just an accident, if Nature is nothing but a drift, and a Darwinian drift at that, then we face one of two conclusions, neither of which is very savory, but both of which are already evident in the unthought-out thinking of the modern world. Human morality in a godless, mechanical universe leads to one of two extremes: either to a mindless humanitarianism or a heartless antihumanitarianism. Either the natural world must absolutely dominate us, or we must absolutely dominate the natural world.

In the one case, says Chesterton, we will reach the point where, more and more, we must keep our hands off everything: not ride horses, not pick flowers, not "disturb the sleep of birds even by coughing. The ultimate apotheosis would appear to be that of a man sitting quite still, nor daring to stir for fear of disturbing a fly, nor to eat for fear of incommoding a microbe." [13] And under this scenario we also must not "disturb a man's mind even by argument". [14]

---

[11] *The Superstition of Divorce*, CW 4:253.
[12] "A Note on Rousseau", *Chesterton Review* 19, no. 4 (November 1993).
[13] *G. K.'s Weekly*, October 25, 1930.
[14] Ibid.

On the other hand, "we might unconsciously evolve along the opposite ... development", the one described by Nietzsche, where everything is used up for our pleasure, with "superman crushing superman in one tower of tyrants until the universe is smashed up for fun".[15]

Here is Chesterton, over a hundred years ago, predicting the two extremes that we see today in the environmental debate: one side saying that the earth must not be touched, that any human action is a blemish on the beautiful skin of Mother Nature, that the natural world would be perfect if there were just no people in it, and the other side sneering and snarling and singing, "Put another log on the fire ..." because we can all have whatever we want, as much as we want, whenever we want it, for as long as we want it. Nature is a bottomless well—a bottomless oil well.

Chesterton's solution to these two extremes sounds suspiciously like common sense. He radically suggests the idea of balance. Proper proportion: on the one hand, "a certain amount of restraint and respect"; on the other hand, "a certain amount of energy and mastery".

> If our life is ever really as beautiful as a fairy-tale, we shall have to remember that all the beauty of a fairy-tale lies in this: that the prince has a wonder which just stops short of being fear. If he is afraid of the giant, there is an end of him; but also if he is not astonished at the giant, there is an end of the fairy-tale. The whole point depends upon his being at once humble enough to wonder, and haughty enough to defy. So our attitude to the giant of the world must not merely be increasing delicacy or increasing contempt: it must be one particular proportion of the two— which is exactly right. We must have in us enough reverence for all things outside us to make us tread fearfully on the

[15] Ibid.

grass. We must also have enough disdain for all things out-side us, to make us, on due occasion, spit at the stars. Yet these two things (if we are to be good or happy) must be combined, not in any combination, but in one particular combination. The perfect happiness of men on the earth (if it ever comes) will not be a flat and solid thing, like the satisfaction of animals. It will be an exact and perilous bal-ance; like that of a desperate romance. Man must have just enough faith in himself to have adventures, and just enough doubt of himself to enjoy them.[16]

It is worth quoting another writer who reflects Chester-ton's thinking exactly:

The believer recognizes the wonderful result of God's cre-ative activity, which we may use responsibly to satisfy our legitimate needs, material or otherwise, while respecting the intrinsic balance of creation. If this vision is lost, we end up either considering nature an untouchable taboo or, on the contrary, abusing it. Neither attitude is consonant with the Christian vision of nature as the fruit of God's creation.[17]

That is Pope Benedict XVI in his encyclical *Caritas in Veritate*.

The world does not understand the earth—because the world has forgotten God. The so-called Green movement cannot see the pitfalls in a philosophy that is trying to save creation without acknowledging that there is a Creator. Ches-terton offers the needed corrective: "The earth is not even earth without heaven, as a landscape is not a landscape with-out the sky. And in a universe without God there is not room enough for a man." [18]

---

[16] Ibid.

[17] Pope Benedict XVI, Encyclical Letter *Caritas in Veritate* (Charity in Truth), June 29, 2009, no. 48.

[18] *The Crimes of England, CW* 5:315.

This is an astounding statement by Chesterton: "In a universe without God there is not room enough for a man." It explains one of the most baffling aspects about the environmental movement, namely, its hatred of people, the attitude that the earth would be just fine if not for the presence of people. The hatred of people is especially evident in the hatred of those people who come in the form of babies, which is another logical somersault. "It is a curious feature of this fad of birth prevention, as distinct from all other fads, that every man professing it ought really to apologize for being alive." [19]

Again, Pope Benedict's encyclical *Caritas in Veritate* reflects Chesterton's ideas and addresses this strange inconsistency among some environmentalists:

> If there is a lack of respect for the right to life and to a natural death, if human conception, gestation and birth are made artificial, if human embryos are sacrificed to research, the conscience of society ends up losing the concept of human ecology and, along with it, that of environmental ecology. It is contradictory to insist that future generations respect the natural environment when our educational systems and laws do not help them to respect themselves. [20]

These environmentalists are trying to restore paradise. But the problem that threw us out of paradise is sin. By not acknowledging Original Sin, they miss the point of what they are doing. The denial of sin leaves them with a very disturbing idea of morality. As Chesterton says:

> A certain sort of humanitarianism or horror of cruelty is almost the only form of morality left among some [of] the modern moralists. There is scarcely anything else they will

[19] *New York American*, May 13, 1933.
[20] Pope Benedict XVI, *Caritas in Veritate*, no. 51.

consent to call a sin, unless it be a sin against a hunted wolf or a crushed cockroach.[21]

But Chesterton avoids the other extreme as well:

No, it is not that the world is rubbish and that we throw it away. It is exactly when the whole world of stars is a jewel, like the jewels we have lost, that we remember the price. And we look up as you say, in this dim thicket and see the price, which was the death of God.[22]

Sin is the problem that destroys the earth. All of creation groans under the Fall.[23] Chesterton is at his most profound when he reflects that all of creation—the earth, the stars, the whole universe—is a precious jewel that has been bought with a price. That price is the death of God.

Christ redeems a fallen world, which includes a fallen creation. Chesterton says that Christ gives us "a sensation that he was turning all our standards upside down, and yet also a sensation that he had undeniably put them the right way up."[24]

Christ renews our astonishment at the universe. Chesterton points out the paradoxical truth that God himself seems to have a sense of wonder. In the climax of the great story of Job, when God finally answers the suffering Job, who has quite understandably been asking for some answers, God gives Job a verbal tour of creation. He starts describing the creatures he has made, like Behemoth and Leviathan. "The maker of all things", says Chesterton, "is astonished at the things he has Himself made."[25]

[21] *New York American*, January 14, 1933.
[22] "The Tower of Treason", in *The Man Who Knew Too Much*, *CW* 8:713–14.
[23] See Romans 8:22.
[24] *Hibbert Journal*, July 1909.
[25] *GKC as MC* (London: Methuen, 1929), 48.

Everything in the creation is precious. Our stewardship of the earth can be understood in mystical terms, so that we are not distracted by the abundance of things, but rather are keenly aware of the unique distinctiveness of each created thing.

> The best and last word of mysticism is an almost agonising sense of the preciousness of everything, the preciousness of the whole universe, which is like an exquisite and fragile vase, and among other things the preciousness of other people's tea-cups. The last and best word of mysticism is not lavishness, but rather a sublime and sacred economy.[26]

In the beginning, God created the heavens and the earth. He called his creation good. He also created a creature in his own image—a creature who could also create images. The proper use of the imagination is to picture what is good, to make things that we can call good. When we use our imagination for sinful purposes, we are abusing one of God's greatest gifts—our imagination, our ability to be creative. Lust, envy, anger, and pride are the sins of the imagination. They are committed by the mind before they manifest themselves in outward action. As God's creative creatures, we also augment creation by being able to see that it is good. And we also augment creation by participating in the creation of more souls who are also creative, and more souls who can appreciate creation. As Chesterton says, every time a baby is born, it is as if God has created a new sun and a new moon, because there is a new set of eyes seeing the sun and the moon.[27]

We defile God's creation when we do not appreciate it, when we do not see that it is good, when we do not put

---

[26] *A Handful of Authors* (New York: Sheed and Ward, 1953), 173.
[27] See *The Napoleon of Notting Hill, CW* 6:374.

things in the right order, when we listen to the snake. Sin
has brought disorder into the creation.

> The point of the story of Satan is not that he revolted against
> being in hell, but that he revolted against being in heaven.
> The point about Adam is not that he was discontented with
> the conditions of the earth, but that he was discontented
> with the conditions of the earthly paradise.[28]

By putting things in their proper order for their proper
purposes, Chesterton gets us to look again at paradise:

> He who has gone back to the beginning, and seen every-
> thing as quaint and new, will always see things in their right
> order, the one depending on the other in degree of pur-
> pose and importance: the poker for the fire and the fire for
> the man and the man for the glory of God.[29]

Our dependence is not on the earth; our dependence is
on God. We can thank God for the earth, as we thank him
for all his good things. The proper perspective toward the
earth is best explained in a lovely reference that Chesterton
makes to Saint Peter—not the Saint Peter who saw the power
of God as he witnessed Christ calming the wind and the
waves, not the Saint Peter who got a foretaste of the new
heaven and the new earth as he witnessed the Transfigura-
tion, but the Saint Peter who saw the world from a different perspective as he was crucified upside down: "I've often
fancied his humility was rewarded by seeing in death the
beautiful vision of . . . the landscape as it really is: with the
stars like flowers, and the clouds like hills, and all men hang-
ing on the mercy of God." [30] It is an everlasting mercy that
we don't fall off.

---

[28] *New York American*, December 15, 1932.
[29] *A Miscellany of Men* (Norfolk, Va.: IHS Press, 2004), 30.
[30] *The Poet and the Lunatics* (New York: Sheed and Ward, 1955), 22.

7

Old and New

The moderns say that they are leaving the past, because it is exhausted; but they lie. They are escaping from the past because it is so strong.

—Illustrated London News, June 1, 1907

The main problem with the modern world is the "modern" part of it, that is, the flat rejection of the past and of tradition, and the mindless embrace of the new and the fashionable and the different—and not just the merely different, but the waywardly different, the abnormal and the diseased. As we noted earlier, G. K. Chesterton says, "A new philosophy generally means in practice the praise of some old vice." [1]

Pope Saint Pius X called Modernism the heresy that includes all other heresies. Chesterton reinforces the same idea by claiming that the best way to tell the tale of modern philosophies and modern thinkers would be as a study in heresies. [2] Whether it is the shunning of the body or the unnatural attachment to the body, whether it is the obsession with form or the escape into formlessness, whether it is

[1] *ILN*, January 6, 1906.
[2] See *America*, March 22, 1930.

anarchy or totalitarianism, materialism or spiritualism, hedonism or puritanism, each of these are modern manifestations of some ancient heresy. It is usually an overemphasis of one particular Church doctrine and a rejection of everything else. The result is a complete loss of balance and perspective: a perfect description of Modernism.

Chesterton says that the modern mind—which is called the modern mind so as to distinguish it from the mind[3]—is "a door with no house to it",[4] "a curious mixture of decayed Calvinism and diluted Buddhism."[5] The modern thinker is a man who combines "an expansive and exhaustive reason with a contracted common sense."[6] Thus, Chesterton suggested that our so-called Modern Age will someday be referred to as "The Muddle Ages".[7]

Though Modernism is a muddle, there are three distinct characteristics by which it can be recognized. First, Modernism is against tradition in general. Secondly, it is against established doctrine and well-defined dogma in particular. And thirdly, it is against thought itself, the reality of ideas and the idea of reality—that is, of a transcendent reality. What these three characteristics of Modernism have in common is that they are all reactionary. Modernism is distinguished more by what it is against than by what it is for. However, it ends up being *for* anything else that is against the same things *it* is against. And so, not surprisingly, Modernism always seems to align itself with anti-Christian philosophies.

When we say that Modernism is against tradition, the natural corollary is that it is in favor of fads and fashions.

[3] See *America*, March 15, 1930.
[4] *DN*, December 11, 1909.
[5] *The Thing*, *CW* 3:226.
[6] *Orthodoxy*, *CW* 1:225.
[7] *ILN*, April 26, 1919.

But it is not so much in *favor* of fads and fashions as that it simply cannot resist them. The modern world does not even know the arguments for tradition, but it immediately gives in to any argument for change.

> This is the only period in all human history when people are proud of being modern. For though today is always today and the moment is always modern, we are the only men in all history who fall back upon bragging about the mere fact that today is not yesterday. I fear that some one in the future will explain that we had precious little else to brag about. For whatever the medieval faults, they went with one merit. Medieval people never worried about being medieval; but modern people do worry horribly about being modern.[8]

Have you ever seen an athlete trying to do a high jump but not making it simply because he did not go back far enough for his running start? That, says Chesterton, is modern thought.[9] Modern philosophers do not go back far enough. Since they do not go back far enough, they do not know what they are taking for granted. They do not know what they are taking for granted, because they do not have the patience to find out. They are too obsessed with the new and the latest and the different—without even bothering to find out what came before . . . or what came first. As Chesterton says, they put first things last.[10]

In our modern muddle, we judge things only by whether or not they are new. The new theologians, says Chesterton, do not worship the sun or moon; they worship the clock.[11]

But what happens to the new things? They become old. "Living in a world that worships swiftness and success no

[8] *ILN*, March 12, 1932.
[9] See *ILN*, July 11, 1914.
[10] See *ILN*, February 15, 1936.
[11] See *DN*, January 25, 1913.

longer means living in a world of new things. Rather it means living in a world of old things; of things that very swiftly grow old." [12]

Tradition is not the worst enemy of Modernism. The worst enemy of Modernism is Modernism. Chesterton points out that religions are killed by their foes, but fads are killed by their followers. [13]

We live in a world of mass communication, where millions of people can be reached instantly with messages that are very polished, very attractive, and very urgent. As a result, people do not hold to the same idea for very long. Opinions are easily swayed, half-truths are easily believed, and worthless theories are easily embraced. Chesterton the journalist saw this coming and warned at the very beginning of the information revolution that the best information is very seldom the latest information. [14] As a prophet, Chesterton has been proved right again and again. He was even prophetic regarding our modern notions about prophets. Nowadays, prophets are heralded for their forward thinking, their progressive ideas, their visionary outlook, their ability to bring the future to us. But the old prophets did not do that. They cautioned us about what the future would be like if we did not repent. They wanted us to think about *today*, and the only tomorrow they talked about was the Day of Judgment. In recognition of their efforts, they were generally put to death.

> The old tragedy of the prophet lay in the fact that everybody disagreed with him. The new tragedy of the prophet lies in the fact that everybody agrees with him. [15]

[12] *ILN*, August 3, 1935.
[13] See *The Outlook*, December 2, 1905.
[14] See *ILN*, January 13, 1912.
[15] *The Bookman*, December, 1934.

> In our existing political conditions, when everybody agrees
> about something, it is generally untrue.[16]

The claim is often made that people have grown indifferent to the creeds of the past because of overfamiliarity.
But, as Chesterton points out, that is not the case. It is just
the opposite. If people are indifferent, it is generally through
complete ignorance of the creeds of the past.[17]

This brings us to the second characteristic of Modernism: it is against doctrine and defined dogma. The moderns
have rejected the creeds of the past, not only because they
are from the past, but because they are creeds. The hatred
of the past includes above all else the hatred of religion.

But Chesterton points out an interesting irony: "Religious belief seems to have an almost morbid attraction for
those who repudiate it as unnecessary."[18] This explains why
the atheist is always thinking about God. And why the modernist, who wants to do away with doctrine, is always thinking about the doctrine he is trying to do away with.
Modernism is particularly obsessed with a rejection of the
Christian creed.

> Nobody ever was required to stand up and say: "I believe
> in Jupiter and Juno," and go on with a fixed and final def-
> inition of all the relations of gods and men. The Creed, in
> that sense, was a Christian thing. And it has proved itself
> indestructible.[19]

Dogma is a dirty word in the modern world. Doctrine is
always seen as something narrow and limited and closed-
minded. But though Modernism rejects doctrine, it has

---

[16] *G. K.'s Weekly*, March 21, 1925.
[17] See *ILN*, September 18, 1920.
[18] *New Witness*, May 19, 1918.
[19] *ILN*, December 31, 1927.

nothing to offer in its place. Every attempt to make something larger than the creed always leaves something out. The modern ideas claim to be expansive and inclusive; they are in fact narrow. They are unable to hold anything so large as Christianity.

The modern hatred of religion is masked with something called tolerance. The modern version of tolerance is the idea that it does not matter what you believe as long you do not really believe it. The problem, of course, with religion is that some people take their religion seriously, and if you have people of different religions believing different things, well, they might argue or something. They might not get along. They might even fight. Therefore, religion is *bad*. And so, if we just throw out the creeds, we'll all get along.

And while we're at it, let's throw out everything that causes divisiveness. There is another old institution that the modern world wants to do away with because it is a thing that separates people, because it is not an open thing but a closed thing, known for its walls and its exclusiveness. What is it? It is the home. It is the family. It is that ancient trinity of father, mother, and child. The modern world wants to do away with this institution, to do away with its very definition, and thereby destroy it—all in the name of unity, of course.

Chesterton saw it coming:

> The scientific and artistic worlds are silently bound in a crusade against the Family.[20]

> A mad notion seems to have got into the modern head that, if you mix up everybody and everything more or less anyhow, the mixture may be called unity, and the unity may be called peace. It is supposed that, if you break down

[20] *The Man Who Was Thursday, CW* 6:508.

all doors and walls so that there is no domesticity, there
will then be nothing but friendship.[21]

> Most of the Utopias represent only a dull sort of destruc-
> tion; the sort of destruction that we call simplification. . . .
> Its cure lies in distribution and even in differentiation; and
> not in mixing up everything together in one great mess
> Nobody seems to have any notion of improving anything
> except by pouring it into something else; as if a man were
> to pour the tea into the coffee or the sherry into the port.
> The modern idea in all human things, from friendship to
> finance, is to pool everything. It is a very stagnant pool.[22]

While the modernists create a muddle, a stagnant pool
that tries to mix everything together without distinction,
they run into a problem. It is impossible to believe nothing. It is impossible to have no dogmas whatsoever. Unless
of course you're a tree. Or a turnip. As Chesterton says,
"Trees have no dogmas. Turnips are singularly broadmind-
ed." [23] There are, he claims, two kinds of people in the
world: those who are dogmatic and know it, and those who
are dogmatic and don't know it.[24] The modernists fall into
that second group. Since they do not define their dogmas,
they are a mass of contradictions, trying to operate without
being willing to acknowledge their own beliefs. They claim
to be more advanced than Christian civilization, they reject
"organized" religion as something artificial, and then they
turn around and indulge in the equivalent of primitive nature
worship, where Mother Nature takes the place of the deity.

---

[21] *ILN*, September 8, 1917.

[22] *Sidelights*, *CW* 21:481.

[23] *Heretics*, *CW* 1:197.

[24] Here is what he actually says: "In truth there are only two kinds of
people, those who accept dogmas and know it, and those who accept
dogmas and don't know it" (*Fancies Versus Fads* [London: Methuen, 1923],
86).

Yet these same people also indulge in very unnatural acts when it comes to sex; contraception and abortion. Chesterton asks, "If Nature herself is so kind a mother, why should anybody be so pessimistic as to shrink from motherhood?"[25] Modernism is a bit mixed up about Nature. Are we supposed to resist it or give into it? "Apparently," answers Chesterton, "Nature is detestable when she commands us to be strong, but infallible when she commands us to be weak."[26]

While the modernists try to do away with meaning, they still have a need for symbols, even if the symbols do not mean anything. We want flags but we no longer want nationalities. We use the institutions of state and commerce to erect gigantic gleaming temples, but we cry out that there must not be any gods. We hold extravagant festivals and pageants in celebration of nothing.

Because we have stopped believing, we have stopped thinking. This brings us to our third point: Modernism is against thought itself. "Modern thought", explains Chesterton, "simply means modern thoughtlessness."[27] He is relentless on this point, supplying example after example.

We talk, by a sort of habit, about Modern Thought, forgetting the familiar fact that moderns do not think. They only feel, and that is why they are so much stronger in fiction than in facts; why their novels are so much better than their newspapers. The current comment on all these things is ... the queerest sort of patchwork of pagan and purely Christian ideas.

For instance, somebody is sure to say in the debate about Decorum: "Is not the human body beautiful?" To which

[25] *ILN*, August 26, 1922.
[26] *The Speaker*, June 23, 1900.
[27] *ILN*, December 14, 1912.

somebody a little more sensible will be quite entitled to answer "No." If he is a ... Socratic philosopher, he will be entitled to answer the question with a question, and say: "Is the hippopotamus beautiful?" The hippopotamus is certainly natural, even if he looks unnatural. He is certainly naked, and accepts no regulations about bathing-tents or bathing-costumes. But the mere fact that he is natural does not make us, in the ordinary sense, admit that he is beautiful. Personally, for my own part, I think he is beautiful; but then, I have a Gothic taste for the grotesque, nourished upon gargoyles. I know what I mean by saying that gargoyles may be beautiful. But the modern materialists do not know what they mean by saying that men must be beautiful.

All that talk about the divinity and dignity of the human body is stolen from theology, and is quite meaningless without theology. It dates from the Garden of Eden, and the idea (which I happen to hold firmly) that God created Man in His own image. But, if you remove that religious idea, there is no more sense in saying that every human being is lovely than in saying that every hippopotamus is lovely. . . .

The old atheists had a theory of life, that could be stated as a connected train of thought. The old theologians had a theory of life, that could be stated as a connected train of thought. But the moderns ... have no connected theory that can be stated at all. Their view of life is a hotch-potch of human and superhuman and sub-human ideas, collected everywhere and connected nowhere. The modern muddler likes to think he is the Superman; likes to think he is the image of God; likes to think as he pleases; but prefers not to think at all. . . . If he would clearly and consistently aspire to beauty, we might ask him to add to it a little dignity. But in fact he has returned to chaos, where there is no asking, nor is there any answer. If man comes out of chaos, by blind evolution or merely groping growth, there is no more sense in calling his body noble than in calling any lump of fungus or cactus noble. If it is noble, it is so by some patent of nobility; and nobility is conferred by a King. But I advise such writers to defer the study of the Body and begin to employ the Mind.[28]

Modernism is marked by skepticism. But skepticism is not thinking. It is doubting. It is the erosion of thought. Thinking involves continuity, which is precisely why, according to Chesterton, modern thought does not qualify as thinking. It is "a series of false starts and belated stoppages. It starts by believing in nothing, and it ends by getting nowhere." [29]

What is most interesting and most telling of all is that while the modern thinkers criticize tradition and Church teaching, they cannot stand being criticized themselves. While they preach tolerance, they are intolerant of any who would dare to disagree with them. Chesterton observes, "Modern thinkers are just like frogs: they are at once jumpy and cold, and they always croak with a curious discordance." [30]

So, we need not be discouraged or even distracted by all the strange new ideas that come along and all the bold new theories that claim to be better than the truths that have been carefully passed from one generation to the other throughout the history of the Church. The old way is still the good way. It is a point repeated by more than one prophet: "Thus says the LORD: 'Stand by the roads, and look, and ask for the ancient paths, where the good way is; and walk in it, and find rest for your souls.' " [31]

The basic truths that our parents taught us as children can be safely taught to our children and to their children.

[28] *ILN*, September 13, 1930.
[29] *ILN*, November 9, 1929.
[30] *ILN*, March 4, 1911.
[31] Jeremiah 6:16.

But best of all, these ancient truths are always a source of comfort in our own lives from beginning to end. We have to strive to keep a continuity with the past, even something so simple as our own past and the innocence of our own childhood. G. K. Chesterton says, "Happy is he who still loves something that he loved in the nursery: he has not been broken in two by time; he is not two men, but one, and has saved not only his soul but his life." [32]

[32] *ILN*, September 26, 1908.

8

East and West

To say that I must not deny my opponent's faith is to say I must not discuss it; I may not say that Buddhism is false, and that is all I want to say about Buddhism. It is the only interesting thing that anybody can want to say about Buddhism—either that it is false or that it is true.

—*Illustrated London News*, October 10, 1908

How many times have you heard someone say, "The religions of the world may differ in their rituals and their external forms, but underneath they all believe pretty much the same thing"? It seems like a nice, inclusive thing to say. But, as G. K. Chesterton points out, there is only one problem with that statement: it is precisely the opposite of the truth. "The religions of the world do not greatly differ in rites and forms; they do differ greatly in what they teach." [1] In most every religion, people pray, they sing, they read sacred texts, they honor their traditions, they have sworn brotherhoods and special feasts, they light candles, and so on. But they do not teach the same things.

---

[1] *Orthodoxy, CW* 1:333.

They do not believe the same things. Chesterton says, "It is exactly in their souls that they are different." [2] Not a very inclusive thing to say. The difference is most profound when it comes to the religion of the East and the religion of the West.

According to the *Oxford English Dictionary*, G. K. Chesterton was the first writer to refer to "Western" man, as in Western culture and Western civilization. He was the first to articulate the idea because he noticed that Western ideas were under attack, though the attack was very subtle. There was a class of wealthy, educated people who claimed to be promoting a more "universalist" religion, a more highly "evolved" religion, by combining the ideas of East and West. But Chesterton could see what they were up to. They were not combining the ideas of East and West; they were simply replacing Western ideas with Eastern ideas. Their claim, according to Chesterton, was "Christianity and Buddhism are very much alike, especially Buddhism." [3]

But if we take an honest look at these two religions, we would see two views of the universe that could hardly be more different. But Chesterton does not merely say that the religions of the East and the West are different. He says one is right and the other is wrong. In his novel *Manalive*, Chesterton introduces us to a larger-than-life character by the name of Innocent Smith, who decides one day that he wants to see what the front of his house looks like. And so he walks out his *back* door and proceeds to walk all the way around the world so that he may walk in his front door. While he is on his journey, he passes through the Far East, where he comes upon a temple and meets a holy man named Wong-Hi. They get into a discussion about a few basic ideas,

[2] Ibid.
[3] Ibid.

such as God and home, and Innocent Smith ends up apol-
ogizing to Wong-Hi. For what? For being right!

Innocent Smith cries, "Your idols and emperors are so
old and wise and satisfying, it is a shame that they should
be wrong. We are so vulgar and violent, we have done you
so many iniquities—it is a shame that we should be right
after all." [4]

The Eastern holy man patiently asks him why he thinks
that Smith and his people are right. The strange pilgrim
answers,

> We are right because we are bound where men should be
> bound, and free where men should be free. We are right
> because we doubt and destroy laws and customs—but we
> do not doubt our own right to destroy them. For you live
> by customs, but we by creeds.... You are steadfast as the
> trees because you do not believe. I am as fickle as the tem-
> pest because I do believe. [5]

The East lives by customs; the West lives by creeds. It is
an important distinction.

But while we are making that distinction, let us also
note how Chesterton goes about comparing the two philosophies. While he claims to be right, he also apologizes
for being right. This is not only his fictional alter ego at
work; this is something that Chesterton himself is known
for. He is always the opposite of arrogant in his defense of
the truth. In his perspective of how East meets West, or
rather, of how East does not meet West, Chesterton
acknowledges that there are honest Buddhists and dishonest Christians, but that is not an argument about which is
the true religion. The modern world does not want to

[4] *Manalive, CW* 7:393–94.
[5] Ibid.

bother with that argument. It asserts tolerance as the ultimate virtue, and thus accepts all error with the charming
idea that even if something is probably wrong, it might
be right. Who's to say? What does it matter, as long as we
all get along? But for Chesterton such tolerance is intolerable because right and wrong, truth and error, really do
matter. It is a matter of life and death, eternal life and
eternal death. So it is important to talk about these things,
and Chesterton demonstrates that it is also possible to talk
about these things *and* get along.

In comparing and contrasting Eastern and Western beliefs,
we find that they are not merely different; they are opposite, just as East and West are opposite. The East is about
oneness and quiescence, the West about separation and surprise. The East is about fate, the West about freedom. The
religion of the East is passive with a resignation and endur-
ance of evil; the religion of the West is marked by an active
hatred of evil and a passion for justice. The goal of Buddhism is nirvana, a state of nothingness, the annihilation of
desire. The goal of Christianity is heaven, being in the presence of God, the complete fulfillment of the heart's true
desire.

Chesterton says that the East is rooted in pantheism, the
idea that God is in everything, that everything is in God,
that everything *is* God. But the West explicitly denies that
idea. Instead of Eastern mysticism's "ecstasy of unity", Christian mysticism is "an ecstasy of creation".[6] And creation is
separation and surprise.

> Buddhism is on the side of modern pantheism. . . . And it is
> just here that Christianity is on the side of humanity and
> liberty and love. Love desires personality; therefore love desires

---

[6] *A Miscellany of Men* (Norfolk, Va.: IHS Press, 2004), 108.

division. It is the instinct of Christianity to be glad that
God has broken the universe into little pieces, because they
are living pieces. It is her instinct to say "little children love
one another" rather than to tell one large person to love
himself. This is the intellectual abyss between Buddhism
and Christianity.... All modern philosophies are chains which
connect and fetter; Christianity is a sword which separates
and sets free. No other philosophy makes God actually rejoice
in the separation of the universe into living souls. But according to orthodox Christianity this separation between God
and man is sacred, because this is eternal. That a man may
love God it is necessary that there should be not only a
God to be loved, but a man to love him. All those vague
minds for whom the universe is an immense melting-pot
are exactly the minds which shrink instinctively from that
earthquake saying of our Gospels, which declare that the
Son of God came not with peace but with a sundering
sword. The saying rings entirely true even considered as
what it obviously is; the statement that any man who preaches
real love is bound to beget hate. It is as true of democratic
fraternity as of divine love; sham love ends in compromise
and common philosophy; but real love has always ended in
bloodshed.[7]

Real love ends in bloodshed. What does that mean? It
means sacrifice. "Greater love has no man than this, that a
man lay down his life for his friends."[8] Jesus said that. And
Jesus did that. Christian love is entirely different from the
pantheism of the East.

The Western mystic, like Saint Francis of Assisi, says, "My
brother fire and my sister water"; the Eastern mystic says,
"Myself fire and myself water."[9] The Eastern attitude can

[7] *Orthodoxy*, *CW* 1:337.
[8] John 15:13.
[9] *Miscellany of Men*, 108.

be described either as "an extension of oneself into everything or a contraction of oneself into nothing." But the effect is the same: it is "always suggesting the unification of the individual with the world." The Western Christian idea is different from that. It is about the separateness of things, the difference of things that allows a relationship between them. "The supreme instance of this divine division", says Chesterton, "is sex." [10] This is why the Church is called the Bride of Christ and why a sacramental understanding of sex is uniquely Christian. "For real love is an intense realisation of the 'separateness' of all our souls. The most heroic and human love-poetry of the world is never mere passion; precisely because mere passion really is a melting back into Nature." [11] In other words, mere passion is mere pantheism. If we merely give into nature, we soon lose the distinction "between sexual passion and sexual perversion". [12]

To follow up nicely on our previous chapter, here Chesterton has identified a surprising twist in Modernism, which in many cases is, not so much old ideas being rejected for new ideas, but Western ideas being rejected for Eastern ideas.

One of the reasons some Westerners are attracted to Oriental religion is that it seems to be more Latitudinarian, whereas Christianity is more doctrinal. Latitudinarian. That's a good word. But what does it mean? The Latitudinarian keeps moving back and forth, trying to avoid boundaries, or erase them. Christianity recognizes the boundaries and has drawn very definite, distinct lines around its categories. It has a very clearly defined creed. But Buddhism, says Chesterton, "is not a creed, it is a doubt." [13]

[10] Ibid.
[11] Ibid.
[12] Ibid., 119.
[13] *The Man Who Was Thursday*, *CW* 6:620.

Christianity has also clearly defined sin. Buddhism avoids such definitions. When someone says he does not want religion to be so black-and-white, so I'm-right-and-you're-wrong, so Thou-shalt-not, it means he is starting to drift East. Such drifters wish, as Chesterton says, "to soften the superior claim of our creed" [14] by giving all creeds the same credence. They are saying in effect that all the creeds are irrelevant. Their supreme virtue is tolerance. The "modern Parliament of Religions", says Chesterton, with its melting together of all the religions of the East and West, is really just a place "where all believers respect each other's unbelief." [15]

The East and the West have very different views of the Fall. The central idea of sin, the awareness of sin, presumes a standard or ideal, not only from which we have fallen, but *to* which we can aspire, or at least appeal. Even though we often fall short, there is a feeling of vigilance, a fight against sin that always keeps us on our guard, and it is precisely this fight against sin, says Chesterton, that "is dangerously absent in Eastern Mysticism." [16]

No two ideals could be more opposite than a Christian saint in a Gothic cathedral and a Buddhist saint in a Chinese temple. The opposition exists at every point; but perhaps the shortest statement of it is that the Buddhist saint always has his eyes shut, while the Christian saint always has them very wide open. The Buddhist saint has a sleek and harmonious body, but his eyes are heavy and sealed with sleep. The mediaeval saint's body is wasted to its crazy bones, but his eyes are frightfully alive. There cannot be any real community of spirit between forces that produced

[14] *Miscellany of Men*, 121.
[15] Ibid.
[16] *The Forum*, June 1929.

symbols so different as that. Granted that both images are
extravagances [but] it must be a real divergence which could
produce such opposite extravagances. The Buddhist is looking with a peculiar intentness inwards. The Christian is staring with a frantic intentness outwards.[17]

Chesterton also points out the difference in the main symbols of each religion. The circle is the symbol of Buddhism, the cross of Christianity. The circle is the symbol of
reason—and madness. Think of the serpent eating its own
tail. The cross is the symbol of mystery—and of health.
Think of the red cross on the side of an ambulance.

Buddhism, he says, is centripetal (spinning inward), but
Christianity is centrifugal (spinning outward): it breaks out.

> The circle is perfect and infinite in its nature; but it is fixed
> for ever in its size; it can never be larger or smaller. But the
> cross, though it has at its heart a collision and a contradic-
> tion, can extend its four arms for ever without altering its
> shape. Because it has a paradox in its centre it can grow
> without changing. The circle returns upon itself and is bound.
> The cross opens its arms to the four winds; it is a signpost
> for free travelers.[18]

Chesterton likes this connection between the sign of the
cross and the sign at the crossroads: "For it is the sign of a
truly Christian thing; that sharp combination of liberty and
limitation which we call choice. A man is entirely free to
choose between right and left, or between right and wrong." [19]

There is also the difference between the Christian idea of
resurrection and the Eastern idea of return. In the East, the
philosophy has to do with the conservation of energy—
some elemental force returns in some form, but the form

[17] *Orthodoxy, CW* 1:336.
[18] Ibid., 231.
[19] *The New Jerusalem, CW* 20:195.

does not return. For some strange reason many people in the West are drawn to what Chesterton calls the romance of reincarnation: "a romance about the soul remaining immortally itself, through the disguises of many different lives." [20] But it is in the Christian West where a much bolder idea is found: "Nothing but the Christian Creed has ever had the audacity to assert that a thing will actually recover its identity because it will recover its form." [21] The resurrection of the body is an idea utterly different from reincarnation.

The Westerners who have been attracted to Eastern religion seem to have a hard time choosing between their desire for reincarnation or their desire for nirvana, the ultimate goal of Buddhism, which is a state of nothingness, the complete negation of desire. This brings up a few practical and moral questions. Chesterton says,

> I willingly believe that any number of Buddhists are very good men, but I cannot see that the theory ... has any particular tendency to make men good. For instance, the Buddhists call Buddha the Lord of Compassion; [but it] seems to me almost the opposite of what Christians mean by charity. The rough, shorthand way of putting the difference is that the Christian pities men because they are dying, and the Buddhist pities them because they are living. The Christian is sorry for what damages the life of a man; but the Buddhist is sorry for him because he is alive. At any rate, he is sorry for him because he is himself.[22]

It is perhaps not surprising that this understanding of Eastern spirituality was precisely what intrigued the German Nihilists such as Schopenhauer and Nietzsche. Chesterton says that Schopenhauer "pursued the impossible paradox of

[20] *ILN*, October 13, 1923.
[21] *The Resurrection of Rome, CW* 21:354.
[22] *ILN*, October 13, 1923.

using cosmic energy in defiance of the Cosmos."[23] The Nihilists with their "frightful universal negatives" arrive at last at final mental collapse, which is what happens to men who are always trying to "find an abstraction big enough for all things."[24]

This idea of the "frightful negatives leading to a collapse" is very prophetic of what would happen in Germany. The Nazis, drawing on Schopenhauer and Nietzsche, were also drawn to Buddhism, even claiming that Buddha was of Aryan origin. Chesterton also points out that the Nazis had adopted for themselves a Buddhist symbol: the swastika, which is an attempt to turn the cross into a circle.[25] And his comments about the circle being a symbol of madness are strangely accurate in this regard.

The Eastern influence would creep West in other ways. Chesterton once wrote a review of a book by an English writer named Aleister Crowley. It was a book of poems that openly demonstrated a sympathy for Buddhism and Eastern philosophy. But Chesterton pointed out that the poems also demonstrated a hatred for Christianity.[26] Crowley denied this. He said he didn't care about Christianity. He was only exploring Eastern thought because he recognized similarities between it and his own agnosticism. There is something typical about this: an agnostic dipping into Eastern thought, denying his hatred of Christianity. He also claimed he had scientific reasons for his agnosticism. Whatever those reasons were, the fact is Crowley's explorations of Eastern mysticism led him to the point where he became an occultist, a heroin addict, and an advocate of sexual perversion, which included homosexuality, pedophilia, bestiality, and

[23] *The Speaker*, November 17, 1900.
[24] Ibid.
[25] See *ILN*, June 11, 1932.
[26] See *DN*, September 24, 1904.

necrophilia. He founded a weird occultist sect called the Thelema Lodge, and its motto was "Do what thou wilt." He was the only man that Chesterton ever refused to debate. Debate is not possible if we do not have some common starting ground. Chesterton had nothing common with someone who was essentially a Satanist. East is east and west is west and never the twain shall meet. Incidentally, other sympathizers with these Eastern sects recruited Crowley to run the Ordi Templi Orientis, O.T.O., the order of the Eastern Temple, a combination of nineteenth-century Freemasonry, Rosicrucianism, and the Illuminati. And one of the American branches of the O.T.O. attracted a young man named L. Ron Hubbard, who remorphed it and founded his own religion, which he called Scientology.

Chesterton uses an evocative image to sum up the difference between Buddhism and Christianity:

> Buddhism seeks after God with the largest conception it can find, the all producing and all absorbing Om; Christianity seeks for God with the most elementary passion it can find; the craving for a father, the hunger that is as old as the hills. It turns the whole cry of a lost universe into the cry of a lost child.[27]

And so the choice is quite clear. There are only two alternatives: East and West—Buddhism and its variations on the one side, Christianity and its variations on the other. Buddhism and Hinduism existed before Christianity. It is possible to imagine them existing if there had never been Christianity. Christianity's distinct claim is that God entered history at a particular time and place. Islam existed after Christianity. It is not possible to imagine Islam if there had never been a Christianity. Chesterton argues (and so does

[27] *The Speaker*, November 17, 1900.

Hilaire Belloc) that Islam is a Christian heresy.[28] Even though
it is very Eastern, it is Western. Eastern Christianity is also
Western. Chesterton points out that Eastern Orthodoxy is
a thing on the borders, just as Islam is. But Eastern Orthodoxy is protecting the borders, whereas Islam is attacking
the borders.[29]

There is one other place and people that fall strangely
between East and West, and at the same time outside of
them. They represent a category that is unique. Because it
is unique it is misunderstood, since it cannot be compared
to anything else. It is a pre-Christian religion that no longer exists as it was, though its people still exist, but the
religion they practice now is not what it was. I am speaking, of course, of the Jews. They are unique, and yet they
are inextricably connected to Christianity, just as Christianity is inextricably connected to the Jews. Jesus and his apostles
were Jews. The Jews made the bold claim to be God's chosen people, but Jesus made the bold claim to be God in the
flesh. And as the Gospel of Saint John says, "He came to
his own home, and his own people received him not." [30]
Jesus founded a Church, and the message that she preached
has been by her own admission, "folly to Gentiles" and "a
stumbling block to Jews".[31] It is also the message that created an abyss between the East and the West.

---

[28] "To do Mohammed justice, his main attack was against the idolatries of
Asia. Only he thought, just as the Arians did and just as the Unitarians do,
that he could attack them better with a greater approximation to plain the-
ism. What distinguishes his heresy from anything like an Arian or Albigen-
sian heresy is that, as it sprang up on the borders of Christendom, it could
spread outwards to a barbaric world." *Where All Roads Lead, CW* 3:53. See
Hilaire Belloc, *The Great Heresies* (1938; repr., Manassas, Va.: Trinity Com-
munications, 1987), 53–96.
[29] See *DN*, June 28, 1916.
[30] John 1:11.
[31] I Corinthians 1:23.

But there was one symbolic moment in history when East did meet West. The Wise Men came out of the East to seek the Christ Child. They did not come to achieve cosmic unity. They came to bow down before the Son of God and the Savior of the world. They recognized a truth that was not within themselves but very much outside of themselves. And they worshipped that Truth. And they presented him with gifts that were distinctly Trinitarian: gold so that he might be crowned as a king, incense so that he might be worshipped as a God, and myrrh because he would be buried like a man.[32]

We have a duty to evangelize the East, and we have to start by evangelizing those here in the West who have taken on an Eastern mentality. It is up to us to be a shining star, so that all men, like the Wise Men out of the East, will follow us to Christ.

[32] See *G. K.'s Weekly*, December 12, 1931.

9

War and Peace

We cannot always at once preserve peace and preserve justice.

—*Illustrated London News*, May 6, 1922

Don't ask me what I think of the war. I will tell you anyway. I won't tell you what you want to hear—that is, I won't tell you whether I am for the war or against it. I will tell you only this: that I think the same way about the war that G. K. Chesterton thinks about the war. Which war? Any war. I defer to his position because, for one thing, curiously enough, it coincides with the position of the Catholic Church.

We all know all the arguments against killing—and even against fighting. The Bible is pretty clear. "You shall not kill." [1] "If any one strikes you on the right cheek, turn to him the other also". [2] "Blessed are the peacemakers". [3] "The harvest of righteousness is sown in peace by those who make peace." (Haven't heard that last one? It's from the Epistle of Saint James, chapter 3, verse 18. And the verses that come

[1] Exodus 20:13.
[2] Matthew 5:39.
[3] Matthew 5:9.

right after it explain why wars begin. You should probably look them up sometime.)

Most people are against war. That's normal. But some of them can be pretty belligerent with their objections. There are some people who object to war because, well, it's violent. But that does not constitute a valid moral objection. As Chesterton points out, if just being physically frightful is the basis of a moral verdict, then there would be no difference between a torturer and a surgeon.[4]

Chesterton says that no one has to be reminded that war is horrible and should be avoided. But here is the question: Is there any justifiable reason to go to war? And here is Chesterton's answer to that question: "The only defensible war is a war of defense."[5] Sometimes the sad truth is that the only way to stop a war is to fight it. Sometimes the only way to stop the fighting is to fight. Sometimes the only way to end a war is to win it—but only as an act of defense, not as an act of aggression. "A real soldier does not fight", says Chesterton, "because he has something that he hates in front of him. He fights because he has something that he loves behind his back."[6]

> A war is not one thing. It is two things which contradict each other.... It is not a corporate act of will, but a conflict of two wills. If one will is trying to do something wicked, the will resisting it is thereby inevitably doing something just.[7]

But Chesterton also points out that it is easy to forget the advantages gained by a defensive war.[8] Say a man knocks

[4] See *ILN*, November 11, 1916.
[5] *Autobiography*, *CW* 16:232.
[6] *ILN*, January 14, 1911.
[7] *ILN*, May 17, 1924.
[8] See *ILN*, April 6, 1929.

another man down and tries to take his wallet. If he succeeds, he will have the wallet to show. But the other man, if he successfully defends himself, will have nothing to show—except perhaps a black eye. He will not have added to the wallets in his possession; he will only have the same wallet he had before. Ironically, disappointment can follow even a victorious war of defense.

But the question is: What are you willing to fight for? Are you willing to fight for your home? Are you willing to shed blood to protect the people and the places that you love? G. K. Chesterton's first novel was a story about a war: *The Napoleon of Notting Hill*. When Chesterton considered why nations go to war, the thing that struck him was that national interests too often mean commercial interests and political interests that have very little to do with the things that are really important in a person's everyday life and with all of the things that he holds sacred. His first foray into fiction is not a story about a war between nations. It is about a war between one suburb of London and the rest of England.

It is interesting to note that the novel is set in 1984, the same year as George Orwell's famous novel. It is remarkable to compare the two visions of a future that is now our past. Both writers foresaw excessive government interference into daily life. But Orwell, seeing a regimental order that would attack the dignity of the individual, paints a picture of despair. Chesterton sees the common man striking back and reclaiming his dignity. Although his novel is bloodier than Orwell's, Chesterton's brushstrokes are graced with hope.

In *The Napoleon of Notting Hill*, England plans to build, through the center of Notting Hill, a commercial roadway system that will destroy most of the small shops and utterly change the nature of the local community. The provost of the district, a young idealist named Adam Wayne, brings his concerns to the king, Auberon Quinn, a somewhat cynical gentleman who doesn't exactly take his role as monarch seriously. But it is precisely because of his detachment that he also does not take seriously his cabinet advisors, named Buck and Barker, who wish to dismiss Adam Wayne. They think Adam Wayne is mad, a dangerous troublemaker, trying to stop "progress", standing in the way of "public interest".[9] The king, on the other hand, thinks Buck and Barker are mad, either mad on money or mad on politics.

But the king is shocked to find that Adam Wayne is actually willing to take up arms to defend Notting Hill. The king finds the idea slightly ridiculous. How can anyone possibly think Notting Hill sacred. Isn't that absurd?

"Notting Hill", answers Adam Wayne, is a "high ground on the common earth, on which men have built houses to live, in which they are born, fall in love, pray, marry, and die. Why should I think it absurd?"

But *fighting* for it? Being willing to die for it? Isn't that a little funny?

Adam Wayne attempts to explain the nature of sacrifice. But he does not take a very soft approach. He begins with the Crucifixion. Now it really is getting serious, and even the cynic is not able to laugh, and now it is Adam Wayne goading the king, daring him to laugh. The king is dumbfounded. Surely this man will not shed blood "for a cursed point of view!"

"Oh, you kings, you kings," cries Adam Wayne with scorn. "How humane you are, how tender, how considerate. You will make war for a frontier, or the imports of a foreign harbor.... But for the things that make life itself worthy or miserable—how humane you are. I say here, and I know well what I speak of, there were never any necessary wars

9 *The Napoleon of Notting Hill, CW* 6:274–81.

but the religious wars. There were never any just wars but
the religious wars. There were never any humane wars but
the religious wars. For these men were fighting for something that claimed, at least, to be the happiness of a man,
the virtue of a man. A Crusader thought, at least, that Islam
hurt the soul of every man, king or tinker, that it could
really capture. I think Buck and Barker and these rich vul-
tures hurt the soul of every man, hurt every inch of the
ground, hurt every brick of the houses, that they can really
capture. Do you think I have no right to fight for Notting
Hill, you whose ... Government has so often fought for
tomfooleries? If, as your rich friends say, there are no gods,
and the skies are dark above us, what should a man fight
for, but the place where he had the Eden of childhood and
the short heaven of first love? If no temples and no scrip-
tures are sacred, what is sacred if a man's own youth is not
sacred?" [10]

A man is sworn to protect his wife and family. He must
protect the place of the family, the place where life is really
lived, which is the home. When men fight to protect their
homes, they fight valiantly and fiercely. When men fight to
take another man's home, they fight coldly and cowardly,
preying on the weak and destroying what is good for something else. The devil cannot create; he can only destroy.

Chesterton illustrates the point about "the twin elements
of loving and fighting" in his marvelous explanation of
romantic fiction. Every story, he says, must have three characters. Saint George and the Dragon and the Princess: "There
must be the Princess, who is a thing to be loved; there
must be the Dragon, who is a thing to be fought; and there
must be St. George, who is a thing that both loves and

[10] If you want to find out what happens next, read *The Napoleon of Notting Hill*, *CW* 6:274–81, from which these quotations were taken (but what
happens next happens after these pages).

fights." [11] All the modern philosophies have tried to do away with this paradox either by substituting fighting for loving, like Nietzsche, or substituting loving for fighting, like Tolstoy. But fighting and loving actually go together. As Chesterton says, "The two things imply each other."

> You cannot love a thing without wanting to fight for it. You cannot fight without something to fight for. To love a thing without wishing to fight for it is not love at all; it is lust. It may be an airy, philosophical, and disinterested lust; it may be, so to speak, a virgin lust; but it is lust, because it is wholly self-indulgent and invites no attack. On the other hand, fighting for a thing without loving it is not even fighting; it can only be called a kind of horse-play that is occasionally fatal. [12]

Thus, according to Chesterton, there is a "natural kinship between war and wooing". [13]

The connection between two such apparent opposites points to the idea that truth is always an amazing balancing act. Balance is the key to beauty, to sanity, to justice. If we lean too far in one direction or the other, we lose our balance. Thus, both militarism and pacificism represent a loss of balance. Militarism is simply bullyism, the strong having their own way. Pacifism is a lack of loyalty, a promise not to defend the innocent, the helpless, the defenseless. Both can be considered cowardly. There is no bravery in being a bully. There is no bravery in refusing to stand up to an enemy. The Church has always had to maintain the precarious balance of truth, whether in war or in anything else. There were times when the Church clearly supported war, and if it had not, we would all be speaking a language right now with a lot more references to *One Thousand and One*

---

[11] *Appreciations and Criticisms of the Works of Charles Dickens, CW* 15:255.
[12] Ibid.
[13] Ibid.

Nights than to *A Midsummer Night's Dream*. There were other times, sometimes surprisingly, when the Church did not support a war and did not support one side or the other in the conflict. Chesterton's image from *Orthodoxy* is striking regarding the Church's ability throughout history to maintain its balance, with "the wild truth reeling but erect".[14]

And he makes another important argument about the Church's historical position with regard to war and fighting. It has to do with the sword. For Chesterton the sword is an important symbol of Christianity. It is not only in the shape of a cross; it is the scriptural symbol of truth, which cuts both ways—because error comes from opposite sides. Chesterton also says he likes swords because "they come to a point", unlike most modern art and philosophy.

The sword, of course, is also connected to knighthood and chivalry. Perhaps Chesterton's most interesting point is that the rise of chivalry, starting in the early Middle Ages, came with the rise of the cult of the Virgin Mary.[15] There is a fascinating connection here. The protection of womanhood and the veneration of the most perfect woman go hand in hand. The rise of chivalry spurred the rise of Western civilization itself, which had to fight continual wars against barbarians who did not have the same respect for womanhood. The passion with which the barbarians fought was lust, whereas Christendom's passion was love.

Against this background, we can see Chesterton's view on war:

> All wars arise from love or lust: the good man loves his country, the bad man lusts after someone else's country.[16]

[14] *Orthodoxy, CW* 1:306.
[15] See *A Short History of England, CW* 20:437, 440–42, 467, 469, 476–77, 532.
[16] *DN*, September 14, 1907.

We do not hold, no sane man has ever held, that war is a good thing. It is better that men should agree than that they should disagree; it is better that they disagree peacefully than that they should fight. The horrors and abominations of war should be avoided. But we also hold that occasion may arise when it is better for a man to fight than to surrender. War is, in the main, a dirty, mean, inglorious business, but it is not the direst calamity that can befall a people. There is one worse state, at least: the state of slavery.[17]

While the possibility of slavery remains, while it merges daily into imminent probability, it is more important to teach men the value of manhood than to preach the softer virtues of peace.[18]

While a good peace is better than a good war, even a good war is better than a bad peace.[19]

How many times have you heard it said that religion has caused the worst wars in history? Well, it is not true. The twentieth century proved that the worst wars in history have been caused by people without religion, by secular states with godless philosophies. Chesterton admitted that of course all wars are horrible, but he accurately predicted that the next war would be the most horrible of all wars. He did not live to see it himself, but his prophecy of World War II was correct. He even foretold that it would start on the Polish border.[20] He said that war in the future will be worse because it will be more cold and calculated, more remote, more impersonal, more indifferent to the individual.[21]

---

[17] *G. K.'s Weekly*, March 16, 1929.
[18] Ibid.
[19] *Everlasting Man*, *CW* 2:333.
[20] See *ILN*, September 24, 1932.
[21] See *ILN*, December 2, 1933.

It is the modern world that has pushed war off the battlefield and into the cities. In a stark contrast to Chesterton's
London suburb fighting a fictional war of independence from
the rest of England, we have seen tyrannical governments
declare war on their own people. We can hardly even call it
war. It is slaughter. Religious wars have been quaint in comparison. And interestingly enough, Chesterton says there
ought to be no war except religious war. If war is irreligious,
it is immoral. No man ought ever to fight unless he really
believes he is right and that his enemy really is wrong, and
he must be willing to present his case to heaven. Unless he
thinks he is eternally and cosmically in the right, he is wrong
to fire a pistol.[22] "If a war is not a holy war," says Chesterton, "it is an unholy war."[23]

He also warns us about the problems of not doing things
for ourselves. When we rely more and more on other people to do things for us, we lose control over our own lives.
This applies to fighting too. Chesterton says that as the
professional soldier gains more and more power, the general courage of a community declines.[24]

The danger of always being prepared to fight is that you
sometimes start looking for a fight. The danger of becoming powerful is that you become too powerful.

> There are three stages in the life of any great power. First it is
> a small power and fights small powers. Then it is a great power
> and fights great powers. Then it is a great power and it fights
> small powers ... but pretends that they are great powers.[25]

So, when the strong is bad it must be opposed. When
the strong is good its greatest strength is restraint. The patriot,

[22] See *ILN*, July 29, 1911.
[23] *ILN*, October 23, 1915.
[24] See *Heretics*, *CW* 1:57.
[25] *Heretics*, *CW* 1:183.

says Chesterton, never boasts of the largeness of his country, but always boasts of its smallness.[26] It all comes back to defending that small, intimate place, the home.

What is the point of war? Chesterton says, "The object of all war is peace." [27] And the object of a religious war is not just material peace, but mental and spiritual peace as well. He argues that if a war is purely political or purely territorial or only for commercial interests, then it aims at superiority. But if it is religious, it aims at equality.[28] It is about coming to agreement. Here is the meaning of loving our enemies. We want to convert them so they are not our enemies anymore. Ultimately, we want to get our enemies to join our side. It may be possible to defeat our enemies, but it is seldom possible to crush them. For as Chesterton says, if you do not understand a man, you cannot crush him. And if you do understand him, very probably you will not.[29]

> Peace will only begin to be possible when we try to do justice to the side with which we do not feel sympathy, and earnestly try to call up in our own imagination the sorrows we have not suffered and the angers we do not feel.[30]

The images of battle and armed conflict are often used to help us understand the spiritual life. The Church on earth is called the Church Militant. War is a metaphor, and it would not work as a metaphor if it were not a reality, a reality that we have to live with. But courage and valor and heroism are better understood by all of us because of the good soldiers who have demonstrated these virtues. And it is a great virtue to stand up for virtue and fight evil that is

[26] See *The Napoleon of Notting Hill*, *CW* 6:288.
[27] *The New Jerusalem*, *CW* 20:360.
[28] See ibid.
[29] See *ILN*, August 18, 1906.
[30] *ILN*, June 25, 1932.

always at war with virtue. The full value of this life, says Chesterton, can only be got by fighting, "because if we have accepted everything, we have missed something—war. This life of ours is a very enjoyable fight, but a very miserable truce." [31]

---

[31] *Charles Dickens, CW* 15:202.

10

Politics and Patriotism

I do not understand America. Nor do you.

—*Illustrated London News*, October 27, 1906

G. K. Chesterton visited America twice. He and his wife, Frances, came in 1921 and again in 1930, spending several months on both occasions, giving lectures to packed houses all over the country.[1] Everyone was charmed and thrilled by his graciousness and wit, some people were certainly baffled by his paradoxes, and a few were actually disappointed—by his size; he did not turn out to be as big as they had expected! He did not live up to his legend in that regard. However, one reporter who was complaining of Chesterton's thinness did make note of the fact that the chair Chesterton was sitting on collapsed during the interview.

The titles of his lectures in America included "The Ignorance of the Educated", "The Perils of Health", and "Shall We Abolish the Inevitable?" The audiences loved them, and the praise of Chesterton was nearly unanimous everywhere he went:

[1] His lecture tour in 1931 included a debate with Clarence Darrow. (See the Appendix.)

There is no man living who can give a truer picture of the follies of the wise. (*Boston Evening Transcript*)

When Chesterton speaks, his voice is heard on four continents. (Edwin Markham, poet, New York City)

He thinks as a twin-six automobile engine runs; looks like William Howard Taft coming back to civilization after two weeks in the woods; and talks like one of his own brilliant essays. (Raymond S. Tompkins, *Baltimore Sun*)

Mr. Chesterton is the most modest man alive. . . . He is one of the best lecturers I have ever heard. (John Crowe Ransom, poet and critic, Nashville, Tennessee)

Chesterton has already produced a library, and still has another one in him. He has written, and well, in all spheres of literature, and about almost everything under the sun. . . . He is the most widely read essayist in the world today. And the reason for this is not hard to find. Most serious writers are so owlishly dull that they make virtue odious and vice attractive. Not so Chesterton. He does not give the Devil all the pretty music of life. He gives the Devil the discords and humanity the harmonies of existence. . . . He is today the world's wittiest philosopher and the world's most philosophical wit. (Martin H. Glynn, Governor of New York)

But what were Chesterton's reactions to America? What did he have to say about us from his unique vantage point as a great English man of letters and a profound observer of human faith and foibles everywhere?

His first impression of America came before setting sail across the Atlantic, as he had to go to the American consulate in London to fill out some papers to get his passport approved. This involved a questionnaire, and one of the first questions was "Are you in favor of subverting the government of the United States by force?" Chesterton's response: "I prefer to answer that question at the end of my tour and not the beginning." [2]

It seems a little unlikely that someone bent on overthrowing the U.S. government would declare his intentions while applying for a passport, but Chesterton found that the inquiry had a sweet transparency to it. Americans, he thought, are the politest people in the world.[3] But declaring one's intentions is, in fact, how America got its start: with a Declaration of Independence.

In declaring that independence, the founding fathers of this country first had to declare the basis for their action. Thomas Jefferson, the author of the document, laid out the axioms very explicitly:

> We hold these truths to be self evident: that all men are created equal; that they are endowed by their Creator with certain unalienable rights; and that among these are life, liberty, and the pursuit of happiness.

Thus, says Chesterton, "America is the only nation ever founded on a creed."[4] He calls it "a nation with the soul of a Church".[5] And even though the nation was founded largely by Protestants, Chesterton maintains that the founding document, the Declaration of Independence, is in its elements a very Catholic document:

> Almost alone among the plans of modern institutions, it bases all government on the right of men to justice, and all rights of men on the authority of God. Though drawn up largely by Deists in what was called the Age of Reason, it

[2] *What I Saw in America*, CW 21:39.
[3] See ibid.
[4] Ibid., 41.
[5] Ibid., 45.

is, compared with most modern philosophies of government, a most papistical document.[6]

In spite of the Christian ideals of the founders, something went awry. Where did the founders go wrong? They
went wrong, says Chesterton, in supposing that it was a
simple matter to realize their ideals. "In other words, they
went wrong, as people generally do, by picking out parts
of the Creed and leaving the rest; by having a clear vision
of human dignity without any comprehension of original
sin."[7]

Nevertheless, in recognizing rights as God given, the
founders recognized the ultimate authority in human affairs.
"Every right", says Chesterton, "is a divine right."[8]

And it might surprise some to learn that he further declares
that the three rights articulated by the Declaration of
Independence—life, liberty, and the pursuit of happiness—
are "the three things to be desired on earth."[9]

It begins, of course, with the *right to life*. It is so fundamental that we are going to discuss it last instead of first—
because everything comes back to the right to life.

We will first deal with the ideal of liberty. In America,
"the Land of the Free", there is an obsession with freedom.
And whenever there is an obsession, there is an abuse, because
something is out of balance.

Liberty can only be understood as freedom within the
rules. This is common sense. As Chesterton says, "Every
sane man recognises that unlimited liberty is anarchy, or
rather is nonentity. The civic idea of liberty is to give the

---

[6] *America*, April 23, 1927.

[7] Ibid.

[8] *ILN*, December 20, 1924.

[9] Interview with Chesterton, "Beginning with Chesterton", *Literary Digest*,
January 22, 1921, 31.

citizen a province of liberty; a limitation within which a citizen is a king." [10]

Two observations made during his first trip to America are especially pertinent:

> The foundation of political liberty is spiritual liberty—the sense that man is an artist and a creator—and that is the real view of the future which a healthy philosophy ought to restore to mankind. The future is a thing which we create out of ourselves as a poet creates a poem.[11]

> Everyone mentions Socrates as a man who dies because he was a bold exponent of new truths, but if you look closer you will see that something else is so. Socrates lived in a world of Sophists, and there were hundreds and hundreds of men proving that there was no God, no conscience. There were multitudes of anarchists around Socrates. He was the conservative who subdued them. He turned sophistry against the Sophists. Socrates is remembered. The rest are forgotten.[12]

Liberty is creative, but it is also conservative. It makes things, but it also preserves things. The real test of freedom, says Chesterton, is the family, "because the family is the only thing that the free man makes for himself and by himself." [13]

And while government is supposed to be the organ of earthly justice to protect liberty, governments have a tendency to start interfering with the rights of the people. For instance to tell a citizen what he can eat and drink is interfering with his rights as a human being. Although Chesterton admires the great freedom in America, he is also stunned

---

[10] *The Superstition of Divorce*, *CW* 4:256.

[11] *Boston Traveler*, January 15, 1921.

[12] *New York American*, February 13, 1921.

[13] *Fancies Versus Fads* (London: Methuen, 1923), 97.

by the lack of very basic freedoms. This was, of course, the time of Prohibition. Though Prohibition was a reactionary policy to an apparent public problem, the Englishman has to explain to his American hosts their misunderstanding about cause and effect:

> There are two kinds of drinking. If a man is happy he drinks to express his happiness. That is good drinking. Then there is the case of the man who is so unhappy that he drinks in the search of happiness. You do not get at the root by stopping his drink. To get at the root you must change the industrial system that makes him unhappy. It is not only to have a more even distribution of wealth, though that would do much. In addition we must bring back old customs, dances, songs, beliefs: the things that kept man happy before modern industry was born.[14]

Chesterton prophetically warns that if a policeman can regulate drinking, there will be nothing to prevent him from regulating smoking, then speaking, then breathing.[15]

In social matters such as this the Catholic Church understands freedom better than the U.S. government does, and certainly better than the fads and fashions that drive the social trends in today's world. The Catholic faith, says Chesterton, "calls for a great deal of self-control in all sorts of people for all sorts of reasons, [but] there are really very few things which it absolutely forbids, as intrinsically and invariably evil; as having no higher form and no possible utility".[16] The short list is devil worship, sexual perversion, a malicious delight in hurting others, and genuine blasphemy that is the cold contempt of God. Sex is lawful in marriage; wine is lawful in moderation; war is

---

[14] *Boston American*, February 12, 1921.
[15] See *ILN*, June 5, 1920.
[16] *Dublin Review*, January–March 1925.

lawful in self-defense; gambling is lawful for those who can lawfully risk the money; and so on. That is exactly where Catholic morals differ from the sweeping negations of the Prohibitionist and the sweeping license of the anarchist. "The Catholic definition is carefully framed for freedom; to allow as much liberty and variety as is consistent with right reason."[17]

Freedom means self-government, which means self-control. It is this concept of self-control that Americans generally do not get. Even though we claim to believe in self-government, we really do not allow it. We are too busy regulating absolutely everything to allow any room for self-government. With the failure of each regulation comes six or eight new correctives. The legislation by the governing classes, says Chesterton, "has become a sort of silly and bewildered experimentation."[18]

Chesterton is rather merciless on politicians, and his stinging observations are amazingly timely:

> Representative government has many minor disadvantages, one of them being that it is never representative.[19]

> The modern representative not only does not represent his constituents—he does not represent even himself.[20]

> Politicians have to live in the future, because they know they have done nothing but evil in the past.[21]

He distributes his blows both left ("The Liberal Party now consists entirely of leaders—or rather misleaders"[22]) and

[17] Ibid.
[18] *ILN*, November 30, 1912.
[19] *Charles Dickens*, CW 15:167.
[20] *ILN*, August 31, 1912.
[21] *ILN*, June 10, 1933.
[22] *The Well and the Shallows*, CW 3:510.

right ("A clock that has stopped is at least right twice a day; the real philosophic Conservative is right with the same regularity as a clock that has stopped" [23]), and both left and right simultaneously:

> The whole modern world has divided itself into Conservatives and Progressives. The business of Progressives is to go on making mistakes. The business of the Conservatives is to prevent the mistakes being corrected.[24]

> The Conservative Party suddenly becomes the Liberal Party the instant it is liberated from responsibility. The Liberal Party suddenly becomes the Conservative Party the instant it has anything to conserve.[25]

> Both modern parties believe in a government by the few; the only difference is whether it is the Conservative few or the Progressive few.[26]

> When Conservatives, Liberals, and Socialists all agree, it is time for the larger and more harmless part of mankind to look after its pockets.[27]

And it was while in America that he made his famous comment: "It is terrible to contemplate how few politicians are hanged." [28] The irony of this gallows humor lies in the fact that it is the politicians who are supposed to be upholding justice that should instead be brought to justice. They should be upholding the right to life, but they have done just the opposite.

[23] *The Speaker*, October 19, 1901.
[24] *ILN*, April 19, 1924.
[25] *ILN*, February 4, 1911.
[26] *What's Wrong with the World*, CW 4:132.
[27] *ILN*, April 5, 1913.
[28] *Cleveland Press*, March 1, 1921.

While the right to life is the most ignored, and the right to liberty the most abused, the right to pursue happiness is the most misunderstood. Obviously the third is dependent on the first two. With no life and no liberty there is no pursuit of happiness.

But what do we mean by this phrase? Like the other terms, it is meaningless without a religious foundation. We are happy only in God. The pursuit of anything else ends in unhappiness.

The Deist who penned the words on the Declaration of Independence may not have known what he was saying, but by asserting basic human rights as God given, he laid the philosophical foundation for the fulfillment of those rights. Life comes from God, and is fulfilled in God ("I came that they may have life, and have it abundantly"[29]). Liberty comes from God and is fulfilled in God ("[T]he truth will make you free"[30]). Likewise, the hunger for happiness comes from God and is fulfilled only in God. We are only happy when we are at peace with God ("You keep him in perfect peace, whose mind is stayed on you"[31]).

The pursuit of happiness has an end: happiness. The pursuit of pleasure does not end in pleasure, because pleasure is not an end. It does not fulfill; it flees. Chesterton warns, "A nation that has nothing but its amusements will not be amused for very long."[32]

We pursue problems instead of happiness when we confuse what is important, when, as Chesterton says, "Our standard of life is that of the governing class, which is eternally turning luxuries into necessities as fast as

[29] John 10:10.
[30] John 8:32.
[31] Isaiah 26:3.
[32] *Chaucer, CW* 18:288.

pork is turned into sausages; and which cannot remember the beginning of its needs and cannot get to the end of its novelties." [33]

Finally, if we think the pursuit of happiness means the pursuit of pleasure, we will soon find ourselves defending vice instead of virtue. This is exactly what has happened in America, where lust is praised as "orientation", greed as "commercial interest", envy as "initiative", anger as "venting", pride as "self-esteem", and so on.

Chesterton points out other particular American weaknesses, that, if they are not vices, they are foibles that we foster. For instance, America, he says, has "a genius for the encouragement of fame." [34] We have seen the cult of celebrity grow completely out of control. He also says that America is the home of lost causes—and strange religious sects, a crude materialism, and even, he says, a crude idealism. [35] "Americans are the most idealistic people in the whole world. Their only danger is that the idealist can easily become the idolator. And the American has become so idealistic that he even idealises money." [36] Chesterton says the typical "real American" is all right. It is the "ideal American" that is all wrong. [37]

The mad materialism in America also tends to encourage cheapness in a way that defies common sense. It is ironic that the American obsession with cheapness is a way for a few exploiters to get very rich. Just as it is ironic that America, which is known for freedom and a pioneering spirit,

---

[33] *Alarms and Discursions* (New York: Dodd, Mead, 1911), 194.

[34] "The Arrow of Heaven", *The Incredulity of Father Brown, CW* 13:47.

[35] See *ILN*, September 13, 1924.

[36] *Tremendous Trifles* (1909; repr., Mineola, N.Y.: Dover Publications, 2007), 164.

[37] *Sidelights, CW* 21:523.

has come to stand for standardization, and what's worse, standardization by a low a standard.[38]

Chesterton makes it clear that he does not hate America, but he does hate the Americanization of the rest of the world. He observes that the trend of the world today is to treat human beings like machines and see how much they can produce. And he points out that this was also the method of the plantation owners of the American South.[39]

This brings up an interesting point. Chesterton notes that America was the last of the great Christian nations to keep slaves. And while modern industrialism and commercialism has reintroduced a form of slavery called wage slavery with a new if similar set of problems, America was also left with another problem unique in the modern world that rose in the wake of slavery. Chesterton found it disturbing that America was the only one of the great Christian nations in which there was a race war, a war, he says, "uncomplicated by any question of religion, undignified by any principle of patriotism, a mere brutal war of breed against breed, of black against white."[40] A Protestant could be killed savagely in Spain; a Catholic could be killed savagely in England. But in these religious persecutions the principle of division was a philosophical principle and was at least the result of some thought-out mental distinctions. But in America, a black man could be killed savagely simply for the color of his skin.

If Chesterton had lived a generation longer, he would no doubt have been gratified to see the barbaric behavior of lynchings come to an end in America, and to see the

[38] See "Culture and the Coming Peril" (lecture, London University, London, England, January 28, 1927).

[39] See *Literary Digest*, January 22, 1921.

[40] *ILN*, February 16, 1907.

country rise up and fight to defend the basic civil rights of all its citizens, regardless of race or national origin. But unfortunately, another very different kind of civil war has broken out since then, not a race war, but a culture war. And in some ways, Chesterton saw this civil war coming too: "A nation is a society that has a soul. When a society has two souls, there is—and ought to be—civil war.... For anything which has dual personality is certainly mad; and probably possessed by devils." [41]

The battle being waged now concerns another group of people who have been denied the first basic human right defined at the founding of this country: the right to life. They are subjected to another barbaric act, as bad as lynching: abortion, the outright slaughter of the unborn. Chesterton saw prophetically that the denial of rights to the unborn is "a denial of the Declaration of Independence. It urges that so far from all men being born equal, numbers of them ought not to be born all." [42]

The first and fundamental right is connected to all the others; in fact it is the reason for the others. As Chesterton says, "The only object of liberty is life." [43]

A true patriot loves his country even when he criticizes it. In fact, it is when he criticizes it that he demonstrates his love, because he wants his country to be better. "A true patriot", says Chesterton, "is always a little sad." [44] "Real patriotism tends to sing about sorrows and forlorn hopes much more than about victory." [45] And of course, Chesterton points out the fallacy in the famous jingoist phrase "My

[41] *Everybody's Magazine*, October 1914.
[42] *ILN*, November 20, 1915.
[43] *Irish Impressions*, CW 20:186.
[44] *The Flying Inn*, CW 7:580.
[45] *The Napoleon of Notting Hill*, CW 6:287.

country, right or wrong." It is like saying, "My mother, drunk or sober."[46]

Patriotism is a local thing, but like anything else, it must have an eternal reference point to have any meaning whatsoever. Our ultimate loyalty must be to our heavenly home rather than our earthly home. But this only makes us take better care of our earthly home: "The more transcendental is your patriotism, the more practical are your politics."[47]

G. K. Chesterton watches America closely. He wants to observe the great experiment of democracy being put to the test. He sees that the real evil of our social estate is not so much that nothing is being done for the people; a great deal is being done. "The real evil is that nothing is being done by the people."[48] The only thing we do is sit around and complain. Chesterton says, "As long as we go on cursing the system the system will be perfectly safe."[49]

Life, liberty, and the pursuit of happiness. These three founding principles of America are under attack. We need to defend life: the unborn, the elderly, the unwanted. We need to restore liberty, which includes the simple freedoms and innocent enjoyments of the common man that have been taken away or else bound up with red tape. And we need to start pursuing happiness instead of unhappiness. We glorify cowboys and truck drivers as representing a rugged American spirit, but what they really symbolize is a lonesome, restless, miserable people. America has become convenience stores and crass commercialism and vast open fields that stretch between incredibly crowded cities. It is

[46] *The Defendant* (London: J. M. Dent, 1907), 125.
[47] *Orthodoxy*, *CW* 1:274.
[48] *DN*, March 12, 1910.
[49] *DN*, January 18, 1908.

not a picture of happiness. As Chesterton says, "Modernist relativism plus Puritan individualism have produced chaos." [50]

Life, liberty, and the pursuit of happiness were the basis of the revolution that formed this country. They are religious principles. They can only be defended based on religious principles. As Chesterton says, "There will be more, not less, respect for human rights if they can be treated as divine rights." [51] And they must be embraced again if we are going to save this country. We need a new American Revolution.

---

[50] *New Witness*, January 20, 1916.
[51] *ILN*, January 13, 1912.

II

Law and Lawyers[1]

When good citizens have at last settled down peacefully
under a law, it generally means that they have found a
good way of evading it.

—*Illustrated London News*, May 17, 1913

G. K. Chesterton would have made an outstanding lawyer.
In fact, I cannot imagine anyone whom I would rather have
as my advocate. He would have argued my case clearly and
thoroughly, taken apart my opponent's case completely and
handily, charmed the jury, and convinced the judge. Though
he would not have proved that I am innocent (because I
certainly am not), he would have demonstrated that the
judge is more guilty than I am and rightfully should serve
my sentence for me. And best of all, the judge would do it
and feel good about it.

There are at least three good reasons why Chesterton
would have made a good lawyer. First of all, he had a passion for justice. If a lawyer does not have that passion, it is
hard to imagine why he should be a lawyer. Chesterton

---

[1] This chapter is largely taken from my article "G. K. Chesterton's Uncom-
monly Sensible Views on the Law", *Ave Maria Law Review* 3, no. 1 (Summer
2005).

championed the causes of the poor and the oppressed, fought for housing, labor, and prison reform, and never failed to point out when the wealthy and powerful managed to avoid justice. Secondly, he demonstrated a keen understanding of the law, from its basics to its fine points. Thirdly, he loved to argue. Not only that, he believed in the benefits of a good argument: "Many people will tell you that nothing has ever come out of arguments. I will tell you that everything has always come out of arguments." [2]

But Chesterton, of course, was not a lawyer. He was a writer. There are any number of reasons why Chesterton was not a lawyer, but certainly one reason is that his strong suit was common sense. This is not to say that lawyers do not have common sense, but they are condemned to hack their way through a jungle of laws that sometimes not only lack in that commodity but even run directly contrary to it.

When laws defy common sense, it is not hard to understand why there is widespread disrespect for the law. The common man disrespects the law because the laws disrespect the common man. This is especially true in America, and Chesterton, an Englishman, saw it very clearly: "In the case of the laws of our American friends it may be said that they break them too easily because they make them too easily." [3]

Chesterton says that courts, judges, and juries produce between them, not a tyranny, but simply an anarchy; "nobody seems to know at any minute whether he is keeping the law or not, or whether or how he will be punished even if he is breaking it." [4] When the law cannot be understood, it cannot be respected. And it cannot even be obeyed. The common man will not even attempt to understand such a

---

[2] *The Poet and the Lunatics* (New York, Sheed and Ward, 1955), 136.

[3] *G. K.'s Weekly*, February 6, 1926.

[4] *ILN*, February 11, 1911.

complicated, many-headed monster. As Chesterton says, he will "learn only enough law so as to avoid the policeman." [5]

How did we get ourselves into such a mess? Chesterton's explanation of the mind-numbing growth of laws in our society is one of the plainest and most profound you will ever hear: "When you break the big laws you do not get freedom. You do not even get anarchy. You get the small laws." [6]

The small laws that are made to mop up after the big laws are broken. The result is that the small laws are given extraordinary attention, while the big laws are not given even ordinary attention.

In one of his most fascinating and creative novels, *Manalive* (half of which is a courtroom drama), Chesterton introduces us to the wonderfully named character, Innocent Smith, who stands accused of attempted murder, breaking and entering, burglary, bigamy, and abandonment. All the evidence is against him, except, as his name suggests, he is innocent.

At his trial, he is defended by Michael Moon, who makes a gallant closing argument:

> Innocent Smith has behaved ... upon a plain and perfectly blameless principle. ... His principle can be quite simply stated: he refuses to die while he is still alive. He seeks to remind himself, by every electric shock to the intellect, that he is still a man alive, walking on two legs about the world. For this reason he fires bullets at his best friends, for this reason he arranges ladders and collapsible chimneys to steal his own property; for this reason he goes plodding round a whole planet to get back to his own home; and for this reason he has been in the habit of taking the woman whom he loved with a permanent loyalty, and leaving her about (so to speak) at schools, boarding-houses, and places of business, so that he might recover her again and again with

[5] *What's Wrong with the World, CW* 4:171.
[6] *DN*, July 29, 1905.

a raid and a romantic elopement. He seriously sought by a perpetual recapture of his bride to keep alive the sense of her perpetual value, and the perils that should be run for her sake. . . .

The idea that Smith is attacking is this. Living in an entangled civilization, we have come to think certain things wrong which are not wrong at all. We have come to think outbreak and exuberance, banging and barging, rotting and wrecking wrong. In themselves they are not merely pardonable; they are unimpeachable. There is nothing wicked about firing off a pistol even at a friend, so long as you do not mean to hit him, and know you won't. It is no more wrong than throwing a pebble at the sea—less, for you do occasionally hit the sea. There is nothing wrong in bashing down a chimney-pot and breaking through a roof, so long as you are not injuring the life or property of other men. It is no more wrong to choose to enter a house from the top than to choose to open a packing case from the bottom. There is nothing wicked about walking round the world and coming back to your own house; it is no more wicked than walking round the garden and coming back to your own house. And there is nothing wicked about picking up your wife here, there, and everywhere, if, forsaking all others, you keep only to her so long as you both shall live. . . .

This man's spiritual power has been precisely this, that he has distinguished between custom and creed. He has broken the conventions, but he has kept the commandments. It is as if a man were found gambling wildly in a gambling hell, and you found that he only played for trouser buttons. It is as if you found a man making a clandestine appointment with a lady at a Covent Garden ball, and then you found it was his grandmother. Everything is ugly and discreditable, except the facts; everything is wrong about him, except that he has done no wrong.[7]

[7] *Manalive*, CW 7:413–15.

As Michael Moon has pointed out, Innocent Smith startles everyone around him because he breaks the conventions and keeps the commandments. The commandments are the big laws. The conventions are the small laws. The key to sanity and salvation, and even good humor, is to keep the commandments and break the conventions. But we have it exactly backwards. As Chesterton says, "Our views change constantly, but our lunch does not change." [8] We have come to the point where our laws are actually contrary to commandments and enforce the breaking of the commandments—abortion, which is murder; no-fault divorce, which is adultery; crass commercialism, which is coveting—but we prosecute little things like paint content and parking tickets and yard clutter and lighting a cigar.

> A scheme of official control which is too ambitious for human life has broken down, and broken down exactly where we need it most. Instead of law being a strong cord to bind what it is really possible to bind, it has become a thin net to cover what it is quite impossible to cover. It is the nature of a net so stretched to break everywhere; and the practical result of our bureaucracy is something very near to anarchy.[9]

Anarchy. The opposite of an ordered society is anarchy. But here's a question: Why is an ordered society based on law preferable to anarchy? The answer should be obvious, but explaining obvious things is never simple. Most of us have not bothered to question our own assumptions or the assumptions that are the foundation on which our society is based. If we did, we might be surprised to discover that

---

[8] *Tremendous Trifles* (1909; repr., Mineola, N.Y.: Dover Publications, 2007), 52.

[9] *ILN*, April 1, 1922.

the best explanation for an ordered society based on law comes from Catholic doctrine.

The very existence of law implies the truth of the doctrine of free will. Obedience or disobedience involves choice, otherwise the words are meaningless. Free will also implies sin. It does more than imply it. As Chesterton says, and as we have often repeated, Original Sin is the one doctrine that can actually be proved.[10] "This sense of sin has made it impossible to be natural and have no clothes, just as it has made it impossible to be natural and have no laws."[11]

The existence of evil, which is evident, implies the existence of good, even when it is not evident. Goodness, Chesterton says, exists independent from the human race, and men either rise to it or fall away from it.[12] The logical conclusion is that natural law, the divine order of things, is demonstrated when it is broken as much as when it is observed. There is a right way and a wrong way to do things. There is an inside and an outside. Freedom exists, not outside the law, but inside the law. The often-criticized "negative morality" of the commandments ("Thou shalt not . . .") actually provides a very wide liberty: "If there are only Ten Commandments, it means that there are only ten things forbidden; and that means that there are ten million things that are not forbidden."[13]

That freedom exists within the law is demonstrated by what happens when we break the law. Doing things the wrong way gets us into trouble and makes things complicated. If it does not land us in a physical prison, it will certainly land us within a psychological prison, a prison of

[10] See *Orthodoxy*, *CW* 1:217.
[11] *The Everlasting Man*, *CW* 2:185.
[12] See *ILN*, May 11, 1907.
[13] *ILN*, October 1, 1932.

guilt from which it is impossible to escape (without the sacrament of penance.)[14]

The Catholic doctrine of free will also implies that we are responsible for our actions. Most civil law relies on the same principle. However, the defense for the lawbreaker often relies on the idea that the defendant is somehow not responsible for his actions. He was insane; he had eaten too much sugar; he had bad parents (and of course, anyone who is a parent knows that this is true). These defenses are all arguments against free will, and they reflect the philosophies that have invaded what was once a Catholic culture. Chesterton, an ardent defender of free will, sees the attack against it beginning with the Protestant heresy of Calvinism, continuing with Darwinism, Marxism, and Freudianism, and a host of other theories that blame our behavior on something else, that our actions are predetermined by God, biology, economics, sex, candy, or getting spanked. All these determinist philosophies are also defeatist. How do we make and enforce laws in such a world? Why should we even bother?

We cannot fully argue these questions without bringing up religion, which means we cannot fully argue these questions because we cannot bring up religion. In modern secular society, we cannot bring up religion, except to say that we cannot bring it up. In spite of that restriction, Chesterton is still able to establish a logical need for law, even apart from the obvious and necessary religious foundation. He does this in discussing the case of a certain activist named Miss Billington, a lady who, as Chesterton explains, "has gone to prison for her political excitability". And here shows why he would make a good lawyer:

---

[14] Chesterton wrote an amazing essay on this topic: "The Macbeths", in *The Spice of Life and Other Essays*, ed. Dorothy Collins (Beaconsfield, Eng.: Darwen Finlayson, 1964), 46–47.

Miss Billington denied that a Court of justice had any authority to try her. The last person who made this modest claim
was, as far as I remember, Charles I: I do not suggest any
similarity in the circumstances or in the sequel. She based
her denial on the ground that the laws are not made by
women, and so should not be enforced on them, which
seems an exhilarating prospect for female poisoners, baby-
farmers, mistresses who thrash servant-girls, and mothers
who kill their children for the insurance. But the essence
of this view of authority was answered long ago, in what
some people call the Dark Ages. It was St. Thomas Aquinas (I think) who pointed out that authority is the same as
authorship—*in auctore auctoritas*. We owe a certain respect
to human society, just as we owe a certain respect to parents, because without them we could not have been. In
merely walking about the street unmolested we are accepting the parental care of the State. The State has given us
life in preventing us from being murdered: without the law,
I might be dead; with the law I must be law-abiding. It is
only on one exceptional and unpleasant occasion that the
policeman comes bodily forward and lays violent hands on
Miss Billington. All the rest of the time the policeman (like
a modest lover) watches unseen over Miss Billington's safety.[15]

The law helps make civilization possible. It is an agreement that usually is practiced without any problem, but occasionally has to be enforced. Chesterton would say it is even
a polite agreement. He explains the connection between
the words "policeman" and "politeness"; they are both connected to the Greek word for city (*polis*). The city (*polis*)
is the "symbol of human civilization". The policeman is

> the representative and guardian of the city ... not merely a
> heavy man with a truncheon: a policeman is a machine for
> the smoothing and sweetening of the accidents of everyday

[15] *ILN*, July 14, 1906.

existence. In other words, a policeman is politeness: a veiled image of politeness—sometimes impenetrably veiled. Politeness is the atmosphere and ritual of the city ... not a thing merely suave and deprecating, but an armed guard, stern and splendid and vigilant, watching over all the ways of men; in other words, politeness is a policeman.[16]

Even those who attack the law recognize the need for the law. Chesterton makes this point in a very amusing manner in his most famous novel, *The Man Who Was Thursday*. The plot involves an undercover policeman infiltrating an underground group of anarchists. It turns out that the anarchists operate according to very strict procedures. They rely on order and obedience, otherwise they would not exist. They are a comical oxymoron: an organization of anarchists.

But the fact that they are anarchists demonstrates they are dissatisfied with the larger order of things. They may have an objection to the law, but they are especially aggrieved by those who flout the law. As one character says, "The poor object to being governed badly, the rich object to being governed at all." [17] This is a problem recognized by even the most conservative commentators on modern civil law, which is constantly abused and tends to be unequal in its application. The law is always fending off anarchy. But the real problem with anarchy is not with the anarchists who are out to destroy the system; the problem is with those who promote anarchy within the system for their own selfish ends.

According to Chesterton, there are two types of people who favor anarchy and actually assist it because they benefit from it: the wealthy elite and the intellectual elite. The

---

[16] *ILN*, September 29, 1906.
[17] *The Man Who Was Thursday, CW* 6:584.

plutocrat favors anarchy because "in anarchy the proudest and greediest person gets on top." [18] The intellectual snob also likes anarchy "because he is not obliged to accept the authority of anything".[19] They both dislike the idea of an intelligible rule that can be applied equally in all cases. In other words, they both dislike common sense. They dislike it because they do not want the law to apply to them. They do not wish to follow the rules. They wish to rule. One wants to be above the law he breaks, and the other, "even more earnestly, wants to be above the law he administers." [20]

In Chesterton's time, this problem was most clearly demonstrated in the case of Prohibition. He marveled that anything as basic and traditional as drinking beer and wine could be outlawed. It was nothing but an attack on a whole culture by a few who did not understand or appreciate that culture. On the other hand, he was not surprised that the pleasures of the poor were attacked, both by the elite who wish to control them and by the rich who have easy recourse to their own pleasure. And the common man, who had no representation in the making of the laws, had no justice in the enforcement of those laws. Prohibition, of course, opened a huge black market for liquor, which enriched a criminal class, while turning the common man into a criminal as well.

Chesterton's provocative musings on law and liberty make us realize that not only would he have been an excellent lawyer; he would have been a great judge—or Supreme Court Justice. As an arbitrator, Chesterton suggests that a judge should not be impartial, but rather, "partial to both

[18] *ILN*, March 23, 1912.
[19] Ibid.
[20] Ibid.

sides".[21] The weakness of the modern judge, he says, is
not that he is partial or impartial but that he tries to be
"ingenious"; after listening to two ingenious theories from
two lawyers, he gives us not "a dull summary of all the
facts, but [creates] some third ingenious theory of his
own."[22] Judges should not do this. They should not have
the power to invent law. For one thing, says Chesterton,
"it encourages legislators to be lazy and leave a bad statute
they ought to repeal."[23] But more importantly, it gives
judges arbitrary power to do away with standards they no
longer recognize because of whatever ideas are currently
fashionable.

> What we call the common sense of our Judges, the way
> in which they mould the law to fit special occasions; the
> way in which a ... Judge will become often a kind of
> benevolent opportunist; all this may be a good thing. But
> it is paternal despotism.... The whole point is, however,
> not that our Judges have a personal power, but that the
> whole world around them, the newspapers, the tone of
> opinion, encourage them to use it in a very personal way.
> In our legal method there is too much lawyer and too
> little law. For we must never forget one fact, which we
> tend to forget nevertheless: that a fixed rule is the only
> protection of ordinary humanity against clever men—who
> are the natural enemies of humanity. A dogma is the only
> safeguard of democracy. The law is our only barrier against
> lawyers.[24]

The flexibility—or humanity—of the judge really should
only come into play when something exceptional arises,

[21] *ILN*, June 25, 1932.
[22] *ILN*, December 9, 1911.
[23] "The Lawlessness of Lawyers", in *The Uses of Diversity* (New York: Dodd, Mead, 1921), 86.
[24] *ILN*, September 22, 1906.

something not foreseen by the law. The problem, however, is that most legislation tries to deal with all the exceptions, which is why so many laws overcome common sense. The rule itself is lost, and we have nothing left but a welter of exceptions.

Although he was neither a lawyer nor a judge, Chesterton did once serve the court in another all-important role: he was a member of a jury. As a result of his experience, he wrote one of his most remarkable essays called "The Twelve Men", which rises to a stunning conclusion.

> Our civilization has decided, and very justly decided, that determining the guilt or innocence of men is a thing too important to be trusted to trained men. If it wishes for light upon that awful matter, it asks men who know no more law than I know, but who can feel the things that I felt in the jury box. When it wants a library catalogued, or the solar system discovered, or any trifles of that kind, it uses up its specialists. But when it wishes anything done which is really serious, it collects twelve of the ordinary men standing round. The same thing was done, if I remember right, by the Founder of Christianity.[25]

Chesterton's warnings to lawyers about the pitfalls of their profession are worth noting. Besides the obvious dangers of accumulating great wealth, the common peril of the legal trade is "its easy degeneration into that of a hired bully and a sophistical butcher".[26] The lawyer's duty is really a sacred one: it is one of service. It is not supposed to be an exercise in gamesmanship and trickery. Chesterton lamented that "representation has become mere misrepresentation; a maze of loopholes." [27]

[25] *Tremendous Trifles*, 58.
[26] *ILN*, August 31, 1912.
[27] *The Crimes of England*, *CW* 5:366.

There are people who fill certain roles in our society who are criticized and made fun of on a regular basis. Among these are priests, mothers-in-law, and lawyers. However, they can withstand the jokes and the criticism because it is obvious that they are permanent; they will always be around. We make fun of them, not because we hate them, but because we rely on them and hold them accountable, something we seldom do with ourselves.

12

Buying and Selling

Let me touch on that terribly delicate matter, the rela-
tion between Truth and Trade.

—*New York American*, July 1, 1933

People are drawn to Chesterton for many different reasons.
But some who are drawn to him for a specific reason are
also driven away from him for another reason. There are
people who feast on his literary criticism but who want
nothing to do with his Christian apologetics. There are people who enjoy his Christian apologetics until it becomes
Catholic apologetics. There are people who like his prose
who hate his poetry. There are people who love his essays
who dislike his fiction. There are people who think he is
right about the Bolshevist Revolution but wrong about the
Industrial Revolution—or prophetically right about the Sexual Revolution but historically wrong about the French Revolution. There are people who crave his detective fiction
but absolutely nothing else. There are people who want
only his quotations and avoid his extended treatment of anything. And, in every case, vice versa. Very few writers present
such a wide range of genres and subject matter to produce
such a variety of reactions, such a mixture of fans and foes

of the very same things. But there is one topic where Chesterton's ideas draw perhaps the fiercest loyalty and also the loudest opposition: economics. This, after all, is not something a man takes lightly, like morality or the fate of the soul. Now we're talking about money!

But even though there are many who would like to compartmentalize Chesterton, it is the thesis of this book that Chesterton is all of a piece, that he is truly a complete thinker, whose ideas are woven tightly together so that his art does not contradict his religion, his politics do not contradict his philosophy, and his economics do not contradict his morality, and so forth.[1] Unlike "the wild divorce court", which is the modern world, Chesterton is the model of a thinker whose thoughts present a happy marriage of ideas, a true unity.

One of the reasons that people who agree with Chesterton suddenly stop agreeing with him when it comes to the topic of economics is that they really do not understand what he is saying—or worse, they do. (Comparisons are odious, but the Pharisees did not understand who Christ was, and the demons did.)

The main problem is that too many readers assume that since Chesterton is a critic of capitalism, then he must therefore be a socialist. They simply do not know that there is another option, which, of course, we will attempt to explain. The minor problem is that there is a famous quotation attributed to Chesterton: "If a man is not a socialist by the time

---

[1] Ironically, this is precisely the argument used by Chesterton's enemies, who feel justified that if they can successfully accuse Chesterton of one incriminating thing, they can then dismiss him altogether. But though they have accused him of many things, they cannot make any of the charges stick. They have never indicted Chesterton. They have only indicted themselves. But as I made clear in the Introduction, I am not going to waste space in this book giving a forum to Chesterton's critics. It was hardly worth making a reference to them in this footnote. Gnats are what they are.

he is twenty, he has no heart. If he is still a socialist when he is forty, he has no mind." Chesterton did not say this. And after years of research, I have come to the conclusion (until someone can prove otherwise) that no one knows who said it. Well, actually lots of people have said it. That's the point. It is a clever antimetabole that has worked its way into the quotation arsenal probably because it reflects a certain gleeful cynicism. But what are we to conclude from this quotation? That the socialist is mindless and the capitalist heartless? Does this somehow make one preferable to the other? It seems like both get disqualified.

The case is further complicated by the fact that as a young man Chesterton did dabble in socialism, as did almost every other young man of his time, living in England on the heels of the Industrial Revolution, breathing its black air and witnessing firsthand its blight, horrified by both the grinding poverty and the obscene wealth it produced. Socialism was the common reaction to capitalism and has remained so, but Chesterton quickly abandoned it when he began his writing career and developed his complete philosophy. Lost in the greater historical shuffle is the fact that capitalism was not originally known as capitalism. It was known as Individualism, which is why socialism, in contrast, was known as socialism. But neither of these social-economic theories have a long pedigree. They are both relative newcomers to the historical stage. And like other modern theories, they have both attempted to enlist science in their service. Chesterton says, "Popular science tries to define realities, and then finds that the definition can be extended to any number of unrealities." [2]

It was no great scientific discovery that man is an animal, and as an animal must eat. But as to how he goes about

_____
[2] *ILN*, March 17, 1923.

getting his food, how content he will be with little food, how satisfied he will be with much food, and what will drive him to acquire more food, along with other stuff that he either wants or needs, as well as all that stuff that he does not want or need, is something that no science can accurately measure and certainly not accurately predict. All of the so-called humane sciences are plagued by the fact that their subject has free will. At some point man will surprise us or disappoint us. And we should know. We do not need an expert to explain this one. In any case, as Chesterton points out, the expert may be right nine times out of ten, "but the tenth time comes." [3]

Economics does not really deserve to be called the dismal science, because even though the subject is truly dismal, it is not science. There is simply no such thing as a purely economic explanation of man. "It is a fallacy to suppose that even buying and selling is economic; for all buying and selling depends upon desire; and desire is the wildest part of the soul." [4]

When Chesterton rejected socialism in the 1890s, he also rejected another school of thought, but this in the realm of art. The catchphrase of Oscar Wilde and the Decadents was "art for art's sake". They claimed to treat art as simply "an ornament of life; neutral in all quarrels ... even the quarrel of life and death". [5] But Chesterton could see that the philosophy of art for art's sake was merely an excuse and a smokescreen for those who wanted to use art for selfish (and often sinful) ends. There was nothing neutral about it. So, too, the idea that economics is purely neutral is a similar fallacy with similar results. Economists tend to create

[3] *Robert Browning* (New York: Macmillan, 1903), 73.

[4] *DN*, October 13, 1906.

[5] *ILN*, March 9, 1929.

man in their own image, or at least according to their own school.

Karl Marx proposed the Economic Theory of History, predicting that capitalism would inevitably lead to communism. And yet, as Chesterton points out, Marx took a major digression from his theory in order to attack religious belief as impeding economic freedom. But if communism is inevitable, how can religion stop it? Why do materialists even bother to discuss religion, much less fume over it? But they do. And in doing so, they shoot themselves directly in the foot.

> Marx gave away the whole Marxian thesis in one sentence; which is perhaps the most famous sentence he ever spoke. He entirely abandoned the Economic Theory of History when he said, "Religion is the opium of the people." In saying that, he took a purely moral influence and made it the origin of purely material action—or inaction.[6]

After exposing Marx as the fraud that he is, Chesterton reveals the fundamental fallacy of the other so-called "scientific" school of economics, which claims that the market is a mere machine. "As there is no perpetual motion in mechanics, so there is no perpetual and self-correcting machine made out of mere economics."[7] It turns out that the capitalists are even more the materialists than the Marxists. "The Capitalist has always held all the heresies of the Communist; including the materialist theory of history."[8]

Capitalism is a system based on labor, where one segment of the society works for another segment of the society, with the latter paying the former a wage. Socialism is also based on labor, where everyone works for the state, and the state pays a wage. Chesterton says,

[6] *G. K.'s Weekly*, January 24, 1935.
[7] Ibid.
[8] Ibid.

There is less difference than many suppose between the ideal Socialist system, in which the big businesses are run by the State, and the present Capitalist system, in which the State is run by the big businesses.[9]

Communism is that form of Capitalism in which all workers have an equal wage. Capitalism is that form of Communism in which the organising officials have a very large salary.[10]

In the days before capitalism and socialism, there was a long and relatively stable period in history where, in most normal towns and villages throughout Europe and even in early America, the majority of men lived lives that did not depend on the wage. They were quite free to marry and have children, they had their own homes, and they had either a field or a craft or a shop. They could buy and sell freely. In the modern world, which has become coarse and strained and quite artificial, even men's normal desires have broken down. They no longer have these normal desires for marriage and property and life itself. "The mere strain of modern life is unbearable; and in it even the things that men do desire may break down; marriage and fair ownership and worship and the mysterious worth of man." [11]

And, as Chesterton points out, in the modern world the common man generally has nothing to sell except his own arms and legs. He is forced to be a laborer because he has no productive property and no independence.[12] "What is wrong is not that there is one class [with] property, but that there is another class without property. What is wrong is

[9] *ILN*, October 27, 1928.
[10] *G. K.'s Weekly*, April 23, 1932.
[11] *A Miscellany of Men* (Norfolk, Va.: IHS Press, 2004), 62.
[12] See *DN*, September 2, 1911.

that this class without property has to hire itself out to the propertied class in order to live at all." [13]

Chesterton knew that capitalism did not work: "Nothing solid can be built on the utterly unphilosophical philosophy of blind buying and selling: of keeping rubbish in rapid circulation like a dust-storm in a desert." [14] But he also figured out that socialism did not work either. It was "the pretence that government can prevent all injustice by being directly responsible for practically anything that happens", [15] and "the fallacy that there is an absolutely unlimited number of inspired officials and an absolutely unlimited amount of money to pay them." [16] He continued to look for a solution to the inherent problem in the modern commercial system that gave rise to disproportionate wealth for the few and disproportionate poverty for the many, a system where men had not only been replaced by machines but reduced to machines, and then discarded like machines. He was looking for that practical balance expressed in Scripture:

[G]ive me neither poverty nor riches;
feed me with the food that is needful for me,
lest I be full, and deny you, and say "Who is the LORD?"
or lest I be poor, and steal, and profane the name of my
    God. [17]

He finally found the solution in the social teachings of the Catholic Church.

When we recite the Magnificat, the beautiful prayer of the Blessed Virgin Mary, we are, surprisingly, describing a

---

[13] *ILN*, November 8, 1921.
[14] *The Well and the Shallows*, CW 3:500.
[15] *ILN*, October 10, 1925.
[16] *The Listener*, November 27, 1935.
[17] Proverbs 30:8–9.

vision of social justice: "He hath put down the mighty from their seat, and hath exalted the humble." [18] Chesterton notes that every social revolution in history has failed solely because it could fulfill only half of the revolutionary maxim of the Magnificat; there have indeed been times when the mighty have been deposed from their seats, but no revolution has ever yet achieved the sequel: exalting the humble, lifting up the lowly. [19]

The Catholic Church has worked to help the poor without something so drastic as a revolution, but with teaching and applying the gospel and transforming lives. It is not simply a matter of performing works of mercy, which provide needed though temporary help. It is a matter of trying to create a just society, to provide a more permanent solution. One of the basic elements of a just society is the just price. The corollary to this is the just wage. It is the principle that those who work are entitled to enjoy the fruits of their labor. And interestingly enough, the Church has recognized that this has especially been a problem in modern society, where too many laborers have not fairly benefitted from their work, even while their work has served to enrich others.

This point was made in the first encyclical on Catholic Social Teaching, which was issued in the midst of the Industrial Revolution, in 1891, by Pope Leo XIII. In *Rerum Novarum* he argued that in order to create a just society, as many as possible should become owners. [20]

Ownership is an ideal. "Thou shalt not steal" would not be one of the commandments if ownership were not an ideal, just as "Thou shalt not commit adultery" would not

[18] See Luke 1:52.

[19] See *New York American*, October 22, 1932.

[20] Pope Leo said that justice should be "distributive", hence, the (awkward) name Distributism.

be a commandment if marriage were not an ideal, and "Thou shalt not kill" would not be a commandment if life were not an ideal, and "Thou shalt not bear false witness" would not be a commandment if truth were not an ideal. So property is normative, like marriage, like life, like truth. Property is proper. Ownership is basic. Pope Leo XIII recognized that this ideal was being abandoned in the modern world, just as there would be attempts to erode the ideals of marriage, of life, of truth. The reason why ownership is important is that it provides independence and protects that basic unit of society: the family. This important principle has been reaffirmed by all of the social encyclicals issued by the popes since Leo XIII, including *Caritas in Veritate* by Pope Benedict XVI.

G. K. Chesterton and Hilaire Belloc and others took Pope Leo XIII's teaching and developed a social and economic movement known as Distributism, something different from both socialism and capitalism. The best way of explaining it is that capitalism is based on individual rights and socialism is based on communal rights, but Distributism is based on family rights and the idea that a society and its economy should serve to protect, nurture, and serve that primary institution consisting of a father, a mother, and children. "As certainly as a brick house is made of bricks, a free state is made of families." [21]

Distributism favors widespread ownership, small businesses, local commerce, and local governance. It is opposed to a remote centralized government just as it is opposed to a remote centralized commercial system. It favors self-employment as opposed to wage slavery. It favors self-sufficiency as opposed to welfare and subsidies. It affirms the principle of subsidiarity, or what the higher orders owe

[21] *G. K.'s Weekly*, April 4, 1925.

the lower orders without superseding the authority of the lower orders. In other words, the common man should be able to control the things that most immediately affect him; he is entitled to make his own decisions, to rule his own household, to decide how to educate his own children, even if the government collects taxes and provides certain services for the public good. The government has a limited role but a necessary role. As Chesterton explains:

> Life is drawn from God, but not from Government; which is, by comparison, only an accidental and even abnormal necessity, arising from the imperfection of life. . . .
>
> There is now a false idealism of turning Government into God, by a vague notion that it gives everything to everybody; to the denial of the liberty given by God, which is called life. . . .
>
> We wish to make the populace creative; whereas practically all modern movements talk in terms of the State creating everything for the populace. A real spiritual abyss only opens when men appear to us to be boasting of bad actions; and this is true of nearly all that modern politicians and philanthropists boast of as their good actions. Social idealism is often actually Satanic; in the quite cold and rational sense that it claims to be the creator. To start the opposite ideal, of creatures being creative, or rather procreative, by a direct authority from the Creator, is not only a difficulty but a risk. It involves the probability of some abuse of freedom in practice. When the abuse is abominable, the true function of Government reappears; which is to exclude extreme abominations.
>
> But if we are to draw up a list of all the cases, for instance, in which a machine must be forbidden because it might be faulty, we must at least be very careful about what authority can correct the fault; and how far that authority may have faults of its own. I do not think it surprising, therefore, if some of those who share this general ideal differ

about the wisdom of establishing this or that law or limitation of liberty.... The new exaggeration is all on the side
of the excessive power of the State; and it is not surprising
that some should seem a little jealous of it, in the struggle
to establish the Free Man and the Family.[22]

Distributism is about that "struggle to establish the Free
Man and the Family". More than capitalism or socialism or
any other social-economic system, it reflects most closely
the social teachings of the Catholic Church.

Truth is consistent, and not surprisingly, the social encyclicals of the popes are consistent, not only with each other,
but with all the Church's teachings on faith and morals. It
is especially worthwhile to note the consistency of the social
encyclicals with another famous encyclical: *Humane Vitae*.
Pope Paul VI saw all the dangers of contraception, not just
to love and marriage, but to the society as a whole. Indeed,
we can now see that it is the contraceptive mentality that is
partly responsible for the myopic nature of modern economics. More wealth actually brings more misery, since
desires that are fruitless and self-serving can never be fulfilled. An economy based on the philosophy of taking as
much as possible cannot work, because there is never any
satisfaction, because there is never "enough".

The contraceptive mentality also lends to the idea of
lending, that is, of building endless debt and never paying
for anything. Take the pleasure and run. A consumer-
driven society that keeps buying but never paying is headed
for collapse. This follows the same mode of insanity
described by Chesterton when he talks about the modern
world that "exalts lust but forbids fertility".[23] It cannot be
sustained.

[22] *New York American*, July 9, 1932.
[23] *The Well and the Shallows*, *CW* 3:501–2.

Yet, anyone who talks about restraint is vilified, whether it is restraint about money or sex, about "free trade" or "free love". But the truth is that neither trade nor love is free. Both require responsibility and discipline. Both require not only investment but sacrifice. Both must abide by prescribed limits. But the modern world finds the idea of any limits repugnant. Freedom is mistaken to mean the throwing off of restraint. But true freedom exists within the rules. Freedom means self-government, which means ruling yourself instead of having someone else rule you. But ruling yourself means self-control.

The argument for Distributism is that it not only involves self-government but self-sufficiency. It means people doing things for themselves. It seems that every time we leave it up to someone else to solve our problems, they do not get solved very well, even when we pay for the solutions. We fall for both socialism and capitalism because we are lazy. We are looking for labor-saving devices. But machines turn even the masters into slaves.[24] And though capitalists claim to hate centralized government, they support the most centralized of all systems when they submit to the industrial system, with its mechanization of everything.[25] The worst danger of labor-saving devices is that we might even fall for the temptation of letting machines think for us, relieving us of the hardest of all work: thinking.

> Just as men feel vaguely that mechanical eyes might not ache with reading, so they feel that mechanical minds might not ache with thinking.... As they would like labour-saving machinery to save them from the hard heroism of arts and crafts, so they would really like another sort of labour-saving machinery to save them from moral science

[24] See *G. K.'s Weekly*, March 21, 1931.
[25] See *ILN*, November 13, 1926.

and philosophy. Their hatred of fixed ideas is like a hatred
of having to build with hard and solid bricks, that really
have to be fitted into each other.[26]

Chesterton is no Luddite who would destroy all machines,
but he does recognize that machines are being used to destroy
people, both figuratively and literally. Under both socialism
and capitalism, people are considered a nuisance, or at best
a statistic for production and consumption.

The more important point is that socialism and capitalism are not only false alternatives to one another, but they
are not really adversaries anymore. They are allies. Socialism
and capitalism are not at war with each other—they are in
cahoots with each other. Big government, which Chesterton calls Hudge, and big business, which Chesterton calls
Gudge, prop each other up. And, as Chesterton argues in
What's Wrong with the World, Hudge and Gudge conspire
together against Jones, the common man.

We see examples of the partnership of Hudge and Gudge
everywhere: the military-industrial complex, which perpet-
uates itself with wars and rumors of wars; the state and
federal highway system that supports the automobile industry; a news industry that has a symbiotic relationship with
the government; bureaucracies that are supported by the
regulation of industry; industries that are supported by government contracts.

We have an economy that is based more on exchange
than on production. Health and education are among our
largest industries and have become so large that they have
had to be nationalized. Huge service industries and finan-
cial corporations have had to be bailed out by the government, not because they were too big to fail, but because

---

[26] *ILN*, March 16, 1929.

they were too big to support themselves. Even farming has become industrialized—and so is subsidized.

And how about this: we used to have in every town a public square, which was a free, open area, not only for buying and selling, but for talking and yelling and arguing (and even smoking). Now we have shopping malls, which are private places for buying and selling, and where people are herded along and kept in line, their voices drowned out by piped-in music, and these giant commercial spaces are underwritten by the state through tax-increment financing.

The vast majority of the population are either wage slaves or bureaucrats. A clerk sitting at a desk does not know the difference if he is working for a large corporation or a large state agency.

In a speech at the University of London in 1927 entitled "Culture and the Coming Peril", Chesterton warns that there is a real evil lurking on the horizon. The peril to man—to his creativity and independent thinking, his ability to contribute positively and productively to his community—the danger to society itself, is not going to be excessive democracy, not excessive vulgarity, not excessive anarchy. It is going to be "standardization by a low standard".[27] And this, of course, is exactly what has come to pass, at all levels of our culture, whether in the state-supported schools or the aisles of packaged trash in the big shops.

It is ironic that in an age of increasing specialization we have lost the one place where specialization was most appreciated: the small shops. I have had the privilege of traveling all across the country giving talks on my favorite writer. While I meet wonderful people everywhere I go, I seldom get to enjoy the unique features of each city and town I visit because the unique features are increasingly

[27] *Chesterton Review* 18, no. 3 (August 1992), 341.

disappearing. Every place looks the same—the same chain stores, the same fast-food restaurants, the same sameness. Instead of local flavor, there is one bland uniform flavor. I have also seen the loss of locality where I live, as the small shops that I used to frequent continue to fold and fail. This is freedom? Where are my choices? I am forced to shop at the big-box retailer, which I lovingly refer to as "The Grand Soviet Distribution Center". Chesterton says, "The big store makes the shop monstrous but the street monotonous." [28]

Ironically, it is capitalism, not communism, that has threatened the world "with the flattest and dullest spread of the commonplace".[29]

> The superiority of the universal shops is a pure superstition. It does not make for better quality in bread or meat that the same shopkeeper should be butcher and baker and candlestick-maker. It only means, if it means anything, the provision of bad candlesticks and worse candles for the inspection of doubtful meat and bread.[30]

Distributism is finally getting some attention, thanks in part to a rediscovery of G. K. Chesterton but also to an economic meltdown that has made people realize that the old economic models are not working. But of course some of the attention it is getting is from those who violently disagree with it. Those who attack Distributism, however, are defending a system that does not work and has never worked.

When I argue Distributism with a socialist, he knows right away that Distributism is not socialism. But he can also figure out that it is not capitalism. However, when I argue Distributism with a capitalist, invariably he will accuse

[28] G. K.'s Weekly, August 3, 1929.
[29] ILN, February 25, 1928.
[30] New Witness, January 13, 1916.

it of being socialism. Ironically, Distributism is much closer to capitalism than to socialism. You could almost say that Distributism is capitalism without the abuse. In fact, the good arguments in favor of the free market are actually defenses of Distributism: productive ownership, entrepreneurship, the freedom to trade and buy and sell, and, more importantly, the freedom to produce.

One critic of Distributism said to me that Chesterton does not like the merchant class. Not true. Chesterton likes the small shopkeeper. He does not like the big shop, which destroys ownership by destroying the small shops and does not seem to be owned by anyone and has wage slaves who do not care about what they are selling. The solution is widespread ownership and more small shops and small businesses and less wage slavery. "A good property system would lessen the exaggerated need of buying and selling, in comparison with producing and consuming." [31]

Chesterton understands and appreciates the role of the merchant class because it performs a valuable service. But there are serious problems in our complex and precarious modern commercial system, and yes, the merchant class has to take a great deal of responsibility for these problems:

> In all normal civilizations the trader existed and must exist. But in all normal civilizations the trader was the exception; certainly he was never the rule; and most certainly he was never the ruler. The predominance which he has gained in the modern world is the cause of all the disasters of the modern world.[32]

There should be a greater emphasis on production than on exchange because that would benefit more people

[31] *G. K.'s Weekly*, June 21, 1934.
[32] *The Well and the Shallows*, CW 3:497.

than the few who are responsible for exchange. It would also prevent the abuse that comes with too much emphasis on exchange. There is too much profit from exchange and not enough from production. This is unjust. It is also unwise.

> The world in which wealth was counted in cherries, and consumed like cherries, was less liable to bankruptcy and despair than that in which we live; which depends on financiers buying and selling cherry-orchards they have never seen and which possibly do not exist.[33]

So, if we may ask in business parlance, what is the bottom line?

> It is the fundamental fact of economics that Business is not fundamental. The fundamental fact is Production; and, first and last, Agriculture. The rock bottom reality on which everything rests is the ploughed field or the plot of vegetables; and these could do without Business better than Business could do without them. The business man is concerned with negotiation and exchange; but he would drop down dead if there were nothing to exchange or nothing about which to negotiate.[34]

Capitalists tend to accuse their critics of suffering from the sin of envy, but oddly enough, they never accuse themselves of perhaps succumbing just a bit to the sin of avarice. But the fact is, greed has obviously given capitalism a rather nasty reputation. Capitalists look silly defending the massive wealth achieved by only a few, pointing feebly to those who fund philanthropic foundations to dispose of the money they were not able to spend during their lifetimes. Chesterton observes: "The weight of wealth disturbs the balance

---

[33] *G. K.'s Weekly*, December 5, 1931.
[34] *G. K.'s Weekly*, March 8, 1930.

of the world even when it is not being actually used against
it." [35]

But capitalists look even sillier defending wealth as the
only motive for enterprise. They argue that there will
be no business without the promise of a great and glitter-
ing reward, the Adam Smith thesis that everyone's selfishness magically works together for the common good, that
as a practical matter, every man wants to get as much as
he can for himself: "Every man must obey his acquisi-
tive instinct." Chesterton says he has seen capitalists use
these as actual arguments against communism and then
act surprised when young people go out and become
communists. [36]

The worship of Mammon, the only alternative god with
any clout, has developed a fairly loyal following throughout history, but especially in the modern world, where the
amount of wealth has increased but so has the disparity
between the rich and the poor. [37] Money, however, is not
a legitimate end. Not only that, says Chesterton, "Money
has no roots.... [I]t is not a natural and familiar power,
but a sort of airy and evil magic calling monsters from the
ends of the earth." [38] The pursuit of money for money's
sake is simply avarice. Greed is not good. The capitalist
argument reveals a fundamental misunderstanding about what
property is for.

> Private property is not a bribe that exists for the sake of
> private enterprise. On the contrary, private enterprise is only
> a tool or weapon, that may sometimes be useful to preserve

[35] *ILN*, January 2, 1926.

[36] *New York American*, January 21, 1933.

[37] This same point is reiterated in Pope Benedict's encyclical *Caritas in Veritate* (Charity in Truth), June 29, 2009.

[38] *Tremendous Trifles* (1909; repr., Mineola, N.Y.: Dover Publications, 2007), 44–45.

private property. And it is necessary to preserve private property; simply because the other name of it is liberty.[39]

In its essence Distributism is liberty—not liberty in the negative sense, that is, freedom *from* something, but rather freedom *for* something, specifically freedom to raise a family without dependence on or interference from Hudge and Gudge. The prerequisite for this freedom is property. As Chesterton says, "Property is really the positive form of Liberty."[40]

G. K. Chesterton is important for many reasons. But perhaps the most overlooked reason is that he is a defender of liberty. It is a word that we all like the sound of, but we seldom think about what it really means. We especially have not been thinking enough about it in modern times, as we have watched every vital freedom erode, as we have embraced various forms of slavery in every aspect of our lives. "It is cheap to own a slave", says Chesterton. "It is cheaper still to be a slave."[41] It seems we trade freedom for security at almost every opportunity.

In America only a century and a half ago, there was a system of outright slavery. We look back at that as not only abominable but intolerable. And yet, most of those who lived under it, and even over it, probably could not have imagined any other sort of society. Perhaps our own imaginations are similarly stunted by our present conditions. We cannot imagine anything other than wage slavery, a system with one class laboring for another class, supplemented by an army of public servants. But there was a way out of slavery once before. There is a way out now.

[39] *New York American*, January 21, 1933.
[40] *ILN*, October 20, 1928.
[41] *ILN*, April 7, 1906.

There is obviously not enough space here to explain everything about Distributism, but the typical question is, how? The first thing is that people have to learn about it, to realize there is another way, a better way. But it means changing their thinking. It means thinking.

G. K. Chesterton devoted the last years of his life to fighting for the poor, to raise them up as in the Magnificat. There were many people—including his own wife—who thought that he was wasting his talents, that he should have been creating more great literature to add to the deposit of immortal words that would sing across the ages. But he could not neglect the poor; he could not neglect the common man, who was his friend. He could not turn his back on those who were crying out for justice. His last Father Brown stories were written solely to support a newspaper dedicated to Distributism. He used his great literary gifts on behalf of the butcher, the baker, and the candlestick maker. And the farmer. Perhaps the value of the battle he was fighting is finally being appreciated.

13

Sickness and Health

If a man's personal health is a public concern, his most
private acts are more public than his most public acts.

—"The Eclipse of Liberty", *Eugenics and Other Evils*

Go lie down. Not for your health. Not even to take a nap.
Go lie down and read Chesterton's essay "On Lying in Bed".
It begins: "Lying in bed would be an altogether perfect and
supreme experience if only one had a coloured pencil long
enough to draw on the ceiling." [1] You will not fall asleep
reading an essay that begins with a sentence so curious and
hilarious as that, even if you are lying in bed.

From his unique perspective of lying in bed and staring
at the ceiling, Chesterton makes a surprising observation:
"If there is one thing worse than the modern weakening of
major morals, it is the modern strengthening of minor morals." [2] This is not something that we might see on the ceiling, but we can certainly see it everywhere else, especially
if we take a look at the prevailing attitudes about health.
We no longer care for the soul, which is eternal, but we

[1] *Tremendous Trifles* (1909; repr., Mineola, N.Y.: Dover Publications, 2007),
49.
[2] Ibid., 51.

spend a great deal of time and energy and money caring for the body, which will soon turn to dust. We worship health. This is not healthy.

Obviously the role of the doctor is to help heal the sick and relieve suffering. This is an act of human compassion. And most doctors follow this vocation for that very reason— they are compassionate people who want to use their talents to help others. But something went desperately wrong when medicine moved from being a vocation to being an industry. The fact is there was a time in our history when most everyone could afford to go to a doctor. Today, if you do not have health insurance, you literally have no business darkening the doors of a hospital. And if you *do* have health insurance, you probably cannot afford that either. Everyone knows that the cost of health care is out of whack, but the only solution being proposed is one we also cannot afford: national health insurance.

It is not a new problem. A National Health Insurance Act was proposed in England in 1912. Chesterton's objections to the Insurance Act were threefold. First of all, it was antidemocratic in practice. The vast majority of the English population were against it. It was being passed against their will, but supposedly for their own good. Secondly, it was antidemocratic in principle. It officially divided the populace into two permanent castes: those who labor, and those who pay for the labor, which amounted to a form of slavery, with one class dependent on the other for its benefits. Thirdly, Chesterton saw the Act as paving the way to the state seizing more power, more influence, more interference in everyone's daily life. Does any of this sound familiar?

The Government thinks less and less of consulting the public. Unluckily, the public also thinks less and less of reforming the Government.... The Insurance Act is not respected: but it is obeyed.[3]

The principle of Compulsory Insurance is that the rich man is forced to buy medicine, but the poor man is forced to take it. This is literally slavery; and begins the claim for entire support on one side and entire obedience on the other. Slavery is scientific, it is workable, it is comfortable; and ... it is intolerable.[4]

It is a good thing to have power to ward off sickness if it should threaten; it is a good thing also to have the power to ward off tyranny if it should be attempted. Both must be fought as well as is possible if they come; and every free man decides the question according to which of them does come.[5]

About a century later, America finds itself looking at essentially the same thing that Chesterton was looking at. We have watched a National Health Care program passed in utter defiance of the public will, rammed through the legislative process with the same "feverish touch" as the Insurance Act in Chesterton's time.[6] We have also watched the entrenchment of a system comprised of employers and employees, of wage earners who are utterly dependent on the system, enslaved rather than being independent and self-sufficient and truly "self-employed" citizens. And we have also watched the unimaginable growth of government as it has insinuated itself into every aspect of our lives.

One of Chesterton's strongest objections to the Insurance Act in his own time was the increase in taxes to those who could scarcely afford to have any of their income taken

[3] *Everyman*, November 21, 1913.
[4] *New Days*, September 18, 1915.
[5] *DN*, August 31, 1912.
[6] See *ILN*, May 17, 1913.

from them, even if it was to be used for something specific, like health care. The tax prevented a man from paying for other needs he had that might be just as important as medical care—or more important.

> Our social reformers today have ... a readiness to grant favours or conveniences to the citizen if he will give up some part of his old independence or isolation as a citizen. The great instance, of course, is the Insurance Act, by which the State professes to smooth and strengthen his protection against certain evils if he will surrender his right to use the money to protect him from other evils.[7]

Chesterton points out that a compulsory Health Insurance Act was first passed in Germany. It followed another compulsory act that was also first passed in Germany: compulsory education. Chesterton is a vocal opponent of state-sponsored, compulsory education for the same reasons he is against a national health insurance. It is an attack on freedom. It gives the government too much power, and it takes away a basic freedom from the citizen. The counterargument is that the state is providing a valuable service. Chesterton's counter-counterargument is that though the state is providing education, it is the state's education. Though it is providing medicine, it is a forced medicine. With compulsory insurance, he argues, people are being forced to pay to be protected against themselves.

People are often willing to trade freedom for security. But the problem is that it is usually someone else trading our freedom for our security—or, for their own security.

Chesterton warns that the state cannot become a universal provider without becoming just another big shop. The one thing we have seen about big shops is that they are

[7] *ILN*, April 12, 1913.

inefficient and unsustainable. They collapse. We can avoid the big collapse if we start getting small again. That would be the cure for what ails the system.

In the meantime, we are suffering the consequences. When we worship health, we begin to redefine morality in terms of health. An unwanted pregnancy suddenly becomes a reproductive health issue that needs to be eliminated. A brain-damaged woman on a feeding tube can suddenly be declared dead while she is still alive. An old and ill person can suddenly be made dead to avoid the nuisance of being left alive.

While the doctor's role is to relieve suffering, sometimes suffering cannot be relieved. As soon as we start prescribing death as a relief from suffering, we are playing God, which is the greatest sin. It is the sin of the devil himself. The Catholic Church has always defended life, which is not always easy to do in a society that worships health. Defending life sometimes means defending suffering.

How did health care get into such a mess? According to G. K. Chesterton, it all started with the term "health care".

> What has health to do with care? Health has to do with carelessness. In special and abnormal cases it is necessary to have care. When we are peculiarly unhealthy it may be necessary to be careful in order to be healthy. But even then we are only trying to be healthy in order to be careless.[8]

Every act of our life cannot be performed with precaution. It cannot be performed with only our health in mind. The healthy attitude toward health is not to think about it at all. We should eat not only because we have a body to sustain but because a meal is a time for a family to sit down together and be thankful and to enjoy each other's company. We should exercise not only because we are trying to

[8] *Heretics, CW* 1:76.

achieve a certain body-fat ratio but because we love mountain climbing or horseback riding or fencing. Sport is a game. The purpose of a game is fun. If we are thinking only about body tissues and muscle fiber, we are missing something. We are missing life. Chesterton says that we should treat our necessities as if they were luxuries. Then we will get much greater enjoyment out of them. "Ordinary things", he says, "are more valuable than extraordinary things." [9] In that sense, every meal, even if it is only broth and bread, is a feast. Every exercise is a dance.

Even a hundred years ago when Chesterton first suggested that health has to do with carelessness, he was taken to task for it. Since science was becoming the greatest authority in society, there was already an attitude that scientific health care professionals were better equipped to take care of us than we are ourselves. Already there was a philosophy of "preventative medicine", which in a sense treats everyone as if he is always a patient, all the time.[10] If everyone is always being treated, it means that everyone is always ill. It means the doctor is ill, too. It is simply the wrong approach to medicine.

> Obviously the real foundation for doctors is not that there is such a thing as health, which they alone know or desire; but that there is such a thing as disease, which they alone have specially studied. You can be an expert in disease. You cannot be an expert in health. Health is too large and free to be explored.[11]

Chesterton is not against doctors. He is against the pervasiveness of "Health Officials", the state control of health,

---

[9] *Orthodoxy*, *CW* 1:249.

[10] "Many hygienic enthusiasts of our time want to think of every man as a patient." *DN*, May 30, 1908.

[11] *DN*, July 6, 1912.

with the government getting involved in every detail of private life. He knows that it will lead to "a long procession of people—all watching each other". And it will, of course, also "be necessary to have somebody watch the official".[12] The obsession with preventative health care can soon turn into complete nonsense.

I know no worse maxim in its practical effects at the present day than the maxim that "Prevention is better than cure." Of course it is strictly true in the abstract. If we could foresee all possible evils a long time before they happened and could modify or avert them without exertion and without harming anything or anybody, obviously of course we should be glad to do so. But this is exactly what is impossible. All our anticipations of the things that are not certain tend of necessity to disorganize the things that are certain. It is possible, for instance, that I may at some time or other catch my finger in a door. The modern professors and scientists, the modern philosophers of hygiene, sociology, eugenics, and all the rest of it, take this possibility and advise me accordingly.

They are divided into two intellectual groups; those who want me to give up doors and those who want me to give up fingers. To take down all the doors in my house, including the front door, would undoubtedly prevent them from pinching me, but I cannot admit that my comfort would really be increased. Chopping off all my fingers with a hatchet would certainly prevent their ever being pinched; but I do not concede in such a case that prevention is better than cure. The whole question touching prevention is whether it does or does not create a morbid atmosphere in attempting to anticipate evil. Does it become miserable through dreaming of misery? For to be always in good health under doctor's orders is only to be an immortal invalid. To be kept always well is really to be always ill. For the essential of the invalid is not danger, which is the pride of the hero, or pain, which is the pride of the martyr; it is limitation, the being tied by the leg to an unnatural life.

Prevention is *not* better than cure. Cure is healthy; because it is effected at an unhealthy moment. Prevention is unhealthy; because it is done at a healthy moment. It is not better that I should always shut my eyes for fear of going blind; it is not worse that I should wait for some sign of blindness before going to an oculist. It is not better that I should prevent a wild buffalo from grazing in my garden by poisoning all the grass. It is much better that I should wait for the buffalo and then endeavour quietly and humbly to *cure* the buffalo— most probably with a gun.

For this reason I have always had an instinct against all the forms of science or morality which professed to be par-ticularly prescient and provisional. Some beautiful idealists are eager to kill babies if they think they will grow up bad. But I say to them: "No, beautiful idealists; let us wait until the babies do grow up bad—and then (if we have luck) perhaps they may kill you." [13]

Chesterton sees a troubling connection between politics and scientifically organized health care: "In both, preventive meth-ods only mean arbitrary power." [14]

There are two opposite extremes into which health care has fallen, both of which combine to make us miserable. And when health care starts making us miserable in order to keep us healthy, we can pretty much conclude that it has failed.[15] At one end is an overly clinical, scientific approach to everything, with a chemical solution to all of life's problems. This makes for an extremely artificial existence.

[13] *DN*, May 30, 1908.

[14] *ILN*, May 17, 1913.

[15] "These great scientific organizers insist that a man should be healthy even if he [is] miserable." *The Ball and the Cross*, *CW* 7:219.

At the opposite extreme is the attempt to make everything natural, to avoid all medical treatment and all technological help whatsoever. But this is also unnatural. It is unnatural to us as civilized human beings.

These two extremes represent two false visions of humanity. One is what Chesterton calls the "Hygienic" view, which tries to create a whole "network of precautions against remote possibilities",[16] so that a man must not drink from a well for want of a filter or let his little girl's hair grow for fear of germs. That is one sort of nonsense. At the other extreme is the idea of merely submitting to Nature in the abstract, to insist that everything be "natural", to regard ourselves as merely passive players in a process that would be perfect as long as we don't interfere with it. Chesterton wants nothing to do with either of these notions.

> I think it foolish to be always guarding against the perils of life, because life itself is a peril. But I think it equally foolish to argue from what life would be if it were never interfered with, because it is perpetually interfering with itself.[17]

Chesterton explains that these two false visions of life correspond to our modern fixation on two periods of time that are utterly vague: "the prehistoric past of which we know very little, and the future of which we know nothing".[18] We fall into either extreme because we have lost our balance. Bodily health and mental health are connected, and both have to do with balance and proper proportion. We have lost that balance because we have lost our sense of what is normal. Old King Cole can no longer call

[16] *DN*, September 11, 1909.
[17] Ibid.
[18] Ibid.

for his pipe and his bowl. And coincidentally, he is no longer a merry old soul. In fact, we could not call him a merry
old soul even if he were merry. We no longer regard people as souls, but as organisms. Materialism has made us forget about the soul and consider only the body. And if a
living body is only tissue without a soul, it can be flushed.

"The mere pursuit of health", says Chesterton, "always
leads to something unhealthy." [19] And the worship of the
body is simply perverse. Look at what it has done to us.
Look at the antismoking laws. Since health has become the
urban god, smoking has been outlawed in bars and restaurants in most cities across America. The reason? Secondhand smoke is a public health issue. But then the smoking
bans have started to extend to parks and sidewalks and other
public outdoor places where secondhand smoke is not an
issue. The reason? Well, children might see it. It sets a bad
example! [20] In a country where abortion is legal and we
pass out condoms in public schools, we worry about smoking in public parks. The small laws. The minor morals.

When health becomes a god it starts speaking through
contradictory oracles. As a principle, it is inconsistently
applied. The health argument reveals the pitfalls of using
science rather than moral principles to establish laws. Science can be just as easily disregarded as it can be invoked
because it has no moral authority. No one dares question
the "scientific studies" about the effects of secondhand smoke,
even though they are questionable. [21] But try bringing up

---

[19] *Orthodoxy, CW* 1:280.

[20] In my hometown of Bloomington, Minnesota, the city councilwoman
who introduced the city ordinance banning smoking in public parks actually
offered this as the justification. Amazingly, only one other city council member objected to this law as being too intrusive on personal freedom.

[21] See Theodore J. King, *The War on Smokers and the Rise of the Nanny
State* (Bloomington, Ind.: Iuniverse, 2009), chapter 8.

the medical evidence about the link between abortion and breast cancer[22] or the irrefutable link between birth control chemicals and deformed fish in America's waterways,[23] and you will be scoffed at as someone who is just looking for a way to interfere with women's rights. Every religion, even the religion of health, has its hypocrites. As Chesterton prophetically observes, "Today it seems that health is preferred to life; and the experts seem to be more satisfied with . . . a well-nourished corpse than with a lively cripple." [24]

He also sees another irony that has arisen out of the worship of health instead of the respect for life: "The success of the Public Health Services has drawn the attention of the theorists to the population problem." The very existence of people is seen as an enemy to health. The more people, the worse it is for health. Thus, population has to be controlled. "It is", says Chesterton, "a logical and obvious economy: Those who are not born will not need the services of the clinic or the doctor." [25]

The hatred of human life is diabolical. It is not pure materialism that has led us to such a state, but it is the wrong combination of the wrong sort of materialism with the wrong sort of mysticism that has led to the unhealthy worship of health. We have plenty of medical miracles, but we are lacking the real miracle of healing because we have combined what Chesterton calls "the sensuality of materialism with the insanity of spiritualism." [26] Recall the Gospel story of

[22] See Karen Malec, "The Abortion-Breast Cancer Link: How Politics Trumped Science and Informed Consent", *Journal of American Physicians and Surgeons* 8, no. 2 (Summer 2003).

[23] See Wayne Laugesen, "'True' Fish Tales: Birth Control and the Environment", *National Catholic Register* 86, no. 20 (September 26–October 9, 2010).

[24] *New Witness*, July 20, 1916.

[25] *G. K.'s Weekly*, February 23, 1929.

[26] *The New Jerusalem, CW* 20:328.

Jesus casting out the demons from the man wandering among the tombs, and sending the demons into a herd of swine.[27] Chesterton says in the modern world we have left something out of that story. We have left out the Redeemer. We have kept the devils and the swine.[28]

The body, as Saint Paul says, is a temple, a temple where the Holy Spirit dwells.[29] The modern obsession with health, however, has made the body a god, and forgotten that is it is a temple. We are supposed to worship *in* the temple. We do not worship the temple. We take care of the temple, certainly, but it is not a funeral chamber. It is a beautiful place full of life. It is a place for feasting and dancing—all for the glory of God.

Chesterton's idea that health has to do with carelessness can be misunderstood. And there are people who insist on misunderstanding Chesterton. He is not advocating a total loss of self-control. In fact, throughout his writings he is always talking about the need for self-control. It applies to our body, it applies to our behavior, it applies to government, it applies to everything. The basis for democracy is self-control, because self-government means self-control. Also, carelessness does not mean indulging in bad habits. It does not even mean acquiring bad habits. Chesterton even says that all habits are bad habits.[30] A habit is a loss of self-control. It means we are doing something, not as an act of the will, but as a thoughtless repetition, something that can only be stopped by a deliberate act of the will. A habit really does mean that our body is controlling us, rather than we controlling our body. A bad habit can get even worse; it can lead to addiction. Addictions are unhealthy.

---

[27] See Mark 5:1–13.
[28] See *The New Jerusalem*, *CW* 20:328.
[29] See 1 Corinthians 6:19.
[30] See *Manalive*, *CW* 7:294.

What Chesterton is trying to do is get us to the right understanding of the human person, who is a combination of body and spirit. If we focus only on the physical, we have lost perspective. If we are only consumed with the spiritual, we also lose touch—literally.

There is a value to be both feasting and fasting, which are physical acts for enlivening our spirits, either by partaking in pleasure or abstaining from it. This is Chesterton's position, and not surprisingly, it is the same as that of the Catholic Church, which has its feast days as well as its fast days. There is a beautiful rhythm to it as the Church weaves the liturgical year with God's own seasons. Christmas is a feast in defiance of winter. Lent is penance during the promise of spring. But fasting, while it may have benefits for the body, is not done for health reasons. It is done for spiritual reasons. It is done to affirm our human dignity, to demonstrate that we are not creatures of mere appetite, and to show that by self-denial we can deepen our appreciation of God's mercy and goodness. Also, the Church has a healthy attitude toward exercise. It is called work. Or, it is called play.

There is, besides work and play, another form of exercise that the Church will encourage on occasion. It is called mortification, which is a very strict, severe way of living in order to keep spiritually focused and to keep one's passions under control. Although some people consider getting out of bed in the morning a form of mortification, it is usually a bit more serious than that. Saint Paul tells us that a Christian is like an athlete running for a prize. Our exercise is not in vain. We are not boxing with the air. In fact, the great Apostle Paul says that he beats his own body to subdue it, to make it his slave.[31] This, of course, is the opposite of today's culture, where we are slaves to our bodies.

[31] See 1 Corinthians 9:24–27.

Those who are called to the religious life do extraordinary things compared to our ordinary things. They take vows of poverty and chastity. But in addition to giving up property and marriage, they also give up other pleasures to which the rest of us can avail ourselves. It is called asceticism. It is usually one of the keys to the mystical life. However, I know of a three-hundred-pound, cigar-smoking journalist who had amazing insight into mysticism, and even asceticism, and had a lifelong devotion to one of the great ascetics, Saint Francis of Assisi. Chesterton says, quite perceptively, that asceticism is a thing that, in its very nature, we tend in these days to misunderstand. It means "the repudiation of the great mass of human joys because of the supreme joyfulness of the one joy, the religious joy".[32] It is the idea that truth alone is satisfying. The mystic, says Chesterton, "passes through the moment when there is nothing but God." [33] How does one know something like this unless he has truly experienced it for himself? Could we call Chesterton a mystic? Yes. Could we call him an ascetic? No. But I suppose that is what makes Chesterton all the more astonishing: that he has achieved such profound mystical insight without the usual accompaniment of asceticism.

In any case, health is not an end, and we lose our proper perspective of life if we make health, not happiness, our goal. Health does not make us happy. Happiness is something we choose, and our ultimate joy comes only from following Christ all the way to heaven.

If we do not have the proper perspective toward health, we will not understand the proper role of doctors. Doctors are servants. They are not priests. In a society that worships

---

[32] *Twelve Types* (Norfolk, Va.: IHS Press, 2003), 34.
[33] *St. Francis of Assisi*, *CW* 2:75.

health, we are in danger of giving the doctor too much power and too much authority. As G. K. Chesterton says, "Over-civilisation and barbarism are within an inch of each other. And a mark of both is the power of medicine-men." [34]

[34] *ILN*, September 11, 1909.

14

Life and Death

The skeptics have no philosophy of life because they have
no philosophy of death.

—*English Life*, October 1924

G. K. Chesterton is often accused of being paradoxical, and,
well, he often *is* paradoxical, but he writes about ultimate
things, and ultimate things are paradoxical. The big truths
are much more than we expect them to be, and they are so
big that they seem to contain contradictions. And few subjects are bigger, more ultimate, and more paradoxical than
death. Chesterton says, "Death is the most obvious and universal fact, but also the least agreeable one." [1]

Skeletons scare us—which is strange, because we all have
one. Chancing upon a stray skeleton in a shuttered room
may cause us to turn in terror and flee, but as a matter of
fact, we are using a skeleton to run away from a skeleton,
and we would be well advised never to run away from our
own skeleton. With a playful reference to the grinning skull,
Chesterton observes, "We think a skeleton is mournful; the
skeleton himself does not seem to think so." [2]

[1] *ILN*, January 13, 1912.
[2] *Alarms and Discursions* (New York: Dodd, Mead, 1911), 168.

And if we do not like to think about death, we like even less to talk about it. Yet it should be the topic most worth discussing. Why? Not because of what leads to death but because of what follows death. "Nothing is important," says Chesterton, "except the fate of the soul." [3]

Perhaps the main reason that no one wants to talk about death is that it is a religious subject. We usually avoid the subject of death just as we usually avoid anything that might be considered "dogmatic". Is there a connection? According to Chesterton, yes.

> Death is a dogma; there is no doubt about death. No Modernist can make death discussable; no Evolutionist can make death vague; no Hegelian can make death life.... King Edward was not partly dead on Friday and faintly alive on Saturday; he was alive and he was dead. Death is not a curve; it is a corner. All death is sudden death.[4]

There is something both objective and subjective about death. Chesterton says, "Death is a positive and defined condition, but it belongs entirely to the dead person." [5]

As with death, so with dogma—there is something that is both subjective and objective about it. Our decision to believe a religious creed may be personal and is of course something that we experience for ourselves even if the truths we embrace are universal and very real. However, if we proclaim something that someone else regards as subjective, it is salted and then thrown out. It is a matter of personal taste and dismissed as such. But when death collides with dogma, it is less easy to dismiss. Would we really make up something like the fear of death? Have we merely invented the dogma of the immortality of the soul? Are sin and guilt

[3] *Appreciations and Criticisms of the Works of Charles Dickens*, *CW* 15:271.
[4] *DN*, May 14, 1910.
[5] *Lunacy and Letters* (London: Sheed and Ward, 1958), 56.

and contrition just in our heads? According to Chesterton,
no.

> Humility and the fear of death and the fixed dogma of
> immortality ... are all ... objective.... The objective truths
> exist, not only outside ourselves, but sometimes in spite of
> ourselves. They are not things men imagine merely for plea-
> sure. In the first case, death and humility are very different;
> but they are both things that many find hard to accept. In
> the second case, the Faith and the Fall are even antagonists;
> but our natural selves are rather reluctant than otherwise, at
> first sight, either to believe that a strain in human nature is
> wrong, or that the authority of a Church is right. Both
> have grand mysteries of consolation behind them; but both
> are too purely objective to be merely optimistic. No man
> merely wants to believe he is infected with Original Sin;
> and no man merely wants to submit to the discipline even
> of an army that will save the world. Primarily we accept
> these truths because they are true; certainly not merely
> because we wished them to be true.[6]

If we continue to examine this nagging connection
between death and dogma, we eventually realize our unconscious dogmas about life. Chesterton gives us an example
of a dogma most of us accept without thinking about
it. We say that a cat gets the better of a mouse, because
we hold the dogma that life is better than death. Unless,
as Chesterton points out, the mouse has read too many
books by German pessimist philosophers, in which case
he would think he had won the race by getting to the
grave first.[7]

And as absurd as that sounds, it is actually a problem in
the modern world. We live in a Culture of Death, an age

[6] G. K.'s Weekly, September 21, 1933.
[7] See DN, November 2, 1907.

of despair where death is often preferred to life. Chesterton crystallizes this somber, morbid outlook: "Our generation, in a dirty, pessimistic period, has blasphemously underrated the beauty of life and cravenly overrated its dangers." [8]

In his great novel *The Man Who Was Thursday*, Chesterton speaks through a character who claims that the worst criminal in the world today is the modern philosopher who hates life itself, his own as much as everyone else's.[9] Thus he defines the Culture of Death long before Blessed Pope John Paul II gave the modern world that piercingly accurate moniker. Chesterton saw it coming, and his writing shows us how the Culture of Death infects today's art and entertainment, our education, our economics, our politics, and our theology. He shows how obviously different things would be in all aspects of our society if we embraced a Culture of Life rather than a Culture of Death.

Let us consider these differences, and let us begin with the obvious one: abortion.

At a time when legalized abortion was unthinkable, Chesterton is already thinking about it, because he sees the way the world is going. He prophetically describes abortion as a "more than usually barbaric form of birth control." [10] It is baby killing, and he says it should "be called by its own name, which is murder at its worst; not only the brand of Cain but the brand of Herod." [11] And he urges us to protest against it, and the protest should be "full of the honour of men, of the memory of mothers, of the natural love of children." [12] Amazingly enough, it was almost a century ago when he said this.

---

[8] *ILN*, May 30, 1908.
[9] See *The Man Who Was Thursday*, *CW* 6:508.
[10] *ILN*, June 3, 1922.
[11] Ibid.
[12] Ibid.

The defenders of the unborn call themselves pro-life, while those who defend abortion call themselves pro-choice. Their two different philosophies are implied in these titles. One side says life is always worth living; the other side says life's worth is just a matter of opinion. One side says death is evil and must be avoided; the other says life can be evil, and that death is the way out. Of course, those who are pro-choice are not defending the choice of the person being killed, but the choice of the person doing the killing.

It is more philosophically sound to defend life than to defend choice, because life is a primary end, and choice is a secondary means. Yes, we believe in liberty, we believe in free will, but what makes free will glorious is choosing what is right, what is good, and what is true. Chesterton's words bear repeating: "The only object of liberty is life." [13]

While abortion is the most obvious example of the Culture of Death, it is connected to a less obvious example that actually paved the way to its acceptance: contraception. Just as the object of liberty is life, so too the object of sex is life. But the Culture of Death has separated these two from each other. Contraception, says Chesterton, "means love towards sex that is *not* towards life." [14]

In his prophetic vision, Chesterton foresees the horror, not only of what we would do to babies at the beginning of life, but of what we would do to the elderly at the other end of life. He says the essence of euthanasia is that we murder people because we fear they may be a nuisance to themselves, but it is a short step to where we murder them because they are a nuisance to us. [15]

---

[13] *Irish Impressions, CW* 20:186.

[14] *G. K.'s Weekly*, March 28, 1925.

[15] See *American Review*, February 1937.

These are hot button topics, of course, that quickly cause division in any political discussion. But Chesterton also shows how politics itself is infected by a dead, materialistic philosophy. We are always hearing, for instance, about the so-called swing of the pendulum, the idea that political trends must go alternately from one extreme to the other. Chesterton says this is "the denial of the whole dignity of mankind". When man is alive he takes a stand. "It is only when he is dead that he swings." [16]

Giving into fashions and trends is not a sign of dignity or of freedom. It is not even a sign of life, but of death. Thus the great Chesterton line: "A dead thing can go with the stream, but only a living thing can go against it." [17]

There is a clear distinction between the philosophy of life and the philosophy of death in our approach to science. There is a huge difference between the man who believes in the soul, in the sense of the will, and the man who only believes in scientific laws to explain all actions and interactions, all deeds, all behavior. "It is a difference of kind," says Chesterton, "like the difference between organic and inorganic matter; or, in other words, between dead things and living ones." [18]

This dead and soulless philosophy has seeped into the language, into the way we talk. Chesterton points out how we speak of the "outbreak of war", as if all the guns blew up without the men touching them. We do not speak of employers paying less or greater wages, which might pin the employers to some moral responsibility; we instead talk about the "rise and fall" of wages. We will not speak of "reform", but of "development". We avoid talking of love

---

[16] *Alarms and Discursions*, 161.
[17] *The Everlasting Man*, *CW* 2:388.
[18] *ILN*, February 21, 1925.

or lust, which are things alive, but instead talk about "the relations of the sexes", "as if a man and a woman were two wooden objects standing in a certain angle and attitude to each other, like a table and a chair." [19]

Thus we teach children how to avoid disease rather than how to value life.[20] We are more concerned with health than with life. Sex has this same soullessness to it, as it has become an exercise in avoiding disease and avoiding life.

A clear distinction can be drawn between the Culture of Life and the Culture of Death in the difference between the way we regard a suicide and a martyr. The modern world does not even understand the difference, sometimes thinking they are the same thing, or otherwise getting it backwards, admiring suicide as somehow a dignified act while dismissing martyrdom as deluded. Chesterton explains the difference:

> Obviously a suicide is the opposite of a martyr. A martyr is a man who cares so much for something outside him, that he forgets his own personal life. A suicide is a man who cares so little for anything outside him, that he wants to see the last of everything. One wants something to begin: the other wants everything to end. In other words, the martyr is noble, exactly because he confesses this ultimate link with life; he sets his heart outside himself: he dies that something may live. The suicide is ignoble because he has not this link with being: he is a mere destroyer; spiritually, he destroys the universe.[21]

In another comparison, or rather, contrast, between the two opposing cultures, Chesterton says, "Living things must constantly be broken up and destroyed; it is only the dead

[19] *Eugenics and Other Evils*, CW 4:325–26.
[20] See *DN*, April 28, 1906.
[21] *Orthodoxy*, CW 1:276.

things that than can be left alone." [22] This brings us to the
Catholic Church. If the Church were dead, as so many people have claimed, there would be no need to attack it and
try to break it up. If it were dead, it would be left alone.
Chesterton gives us another corollary: "People will tell you
that theology became too elaborate because it was dead.
Believe me, if it had been dead it would never have become
elaborate; it is only the live tree that grows too many
branches." [23] So, too, tradition, which some call a dead thing,
is something very much alive, that outlives us and our "mad
little movements". [24]

Interestingly enough, one of the most important traditions in a sane society is the way we treat the dead. Funeral
traditions are all about human dignity. Chesterton says that
even in an empire of atheists the dead man is sacred. "It is
a strange and amusing fact that even the materialists who
believe that death does nothing except turn a fellow-
creature into refuse, only begin to reverence a fellow-
creature at the moment that he has been turned into
refuse." [25] And yet the modern cult of hygiene that prefers
health to life has lost the ancient reverence for death that
was shared with us even by atheists. Chesterton accurately
predicts that the cult of hygiene would lead to an insistence
on cremation rather than burial. [26] If the dying are a nuisance, the dead are even a greater nuisance. As a way of
denying death, we deny the existence of the dead. We
deny them their place. A cemetery reminds us that we will
die. Scattered ashes we forget about. So, too, the word

[22] *Lunacy and Letters*, 173.
[23] *Tremendous Trifles* (1909; repr., Mineola, N.Y.: Dover Publications, 2007), 109.
[24] *The Man Who Was Thursday*, *CW* 6:510.
[25] *Lunacy and Letters*, 30.
[26] See *Dublin Review*, October 1910.

"undertaker" is a modern euphemism. It means that we need not think about such things, because there is some slave who will undertake *It*—that is, who will take *It* away.[27] The word "mortician" is more modern and perhaps more accurate, but it has a clean, clinical, scientific ring to it, and it still gets between us and the reality of death.

We are not facing death, says Chesterton, because we are "not facing life as it is; life as it is, is almost too splendid—nay, too beautiful to be faced."[28]

Why do we fear death? It is perfectly natural. But beyond any survival instinct, any dread of the unknown, it is not death that we fear so much as judgment. More specifically, it is not death we fear but hell. The most natural fear is the fear of falling, and hell, says Chesterton, is "an infinity of falling".[29]

There is a solution to this problem, you know. The gospel, the good news, is the promise of eternal life. We know we do not want to go to hell, which is eternal death. We know we want to go to heaven, which is eternal life. It is the reality of death that makes life so valuable, that points not merely to our *desire* for eternal life, but to the fact that we were all *designed* for eternal life. We were made for communion with God. Something broke that communion. Something else restored that communion. It is only the curse we all share that makes us think about the promise that also belongs to all of us. Chesterton says, "Only where death and eternity are intensely present can human beings fully feel their fellowship."[30]

Only death can make us think about eternal life. But it also has the salubrious effect of making us think of this life

[27] See *New Witness*, January 20, 1916.
[28] *ILN*, March 12, 1910.
[29] *Lunacy and Letters*, 157.
[30] *The Victorian Age in Literature*, *CW* 15:462–63.

here and now. "Life is always worth living while men feel that they may die." [31] It is why Chesterton carried a gun— not to kill anyone but to make a person gain a greater appreciation of life should he have the bad judgment to complain that life is not worth living. It is a comment one reconsiders when staring down the barrel of a gun.

> It is the point of all deprivation that it sharpens the idea of value; and, perhaps, this is, after all, the reason of the riddle of death. In a better world, perhaps, we may permanently possess, and permanently be astonished at possession. In some strange estate beyond the stars we may manage at once to have and to enjoy. But in this world, through some sickness at the root of psychology, we have to be reminded that a thing is ours by its power of disappearance. With us the prize of life is one great, glorious cry of the dying; it is always *morituri te salutant.* ("We about to die salute you.") At the four corners of our human temple of happiness stand a lame man pointing to one road, and a blind man worshipping the sun, a deaf man listening for the birds, and a dead man thanking God for his creation.[32]

Though Chesterton says that death "is distinctly an exciting moment",[33] and it is the dying that makes life dramatic, we must not forget: "Life after all is much more dramatic than death." [34]

As pointed out earlier, we do not want to face either of the great realities of death and dogma. Even though we admit that mortal reality, we do not want to admit religious reality. But it is real—as real as death, and more importantly, as real as life.

---

[31] *Alarms and Discursions,* 170.
[32] *Lunacy and Letters,* 16–17.
[33] *Orthodoxy, CW* 1:241.
[34] *Time's Abstract and Brief Chronicle, CW* 11:82.

Religion is revelation. In other words, it is a vision, and a vision received by faith; but it is a vision of reality. The faith consists in a conviction of its reality. It is not a mythology, neither is it a philosophy. It is not a philosophy because, being a vision, it is not a pattern but a picture. It is not one of those abstract explanations that attempt to resolve everything with a simplification: that everything is relative; or everything is recurrent; or everything is inevitable; or everything is an illusion. It is not a process but a picture. It is not a process, but a story. It is as convincing as a picture or a story is convincing. In other words, it is exactly, as the phrase goes, like life. For indeed it is life.[35]

Jesus said that he came that we might have life and have it more abundantly.[36] Eternal life does not merely mean endless life—although it *does* mean that—it means life to the fullest, life overflowing. It was God's great gift at creation, a gift destroyed by sin, but restored by Christ. It is sacred. Life is sacred. Chesterton says, more prophetically than he could have possibly known, that among all the cosmic creeds, the Catholic faith "is the only one that is entirely on the side of Life." [37] But he also says that if we believe in the sanctity of human life, it must be really a sanctity, and we must be prepared to make sacrifices for it.[38] Paradoxically, we may be called, like Christ, to die on behalf of life.

People sometimes wonder how men come to fight about their opinions; to fight until blood runs down the gutters. The explanation is really quite simple; it is that any dispute becomes ultimately a dispute about common sense. And they always discover that common sense is the one thing that they have not got in common. The great misfortune

[35] *The Everlasting Man, CW* 2:376.
[36] See John 10:10.
[37] *St. Thomas Aquinas, CW* 2:490.
[38] See *DN*, December 13, 1901.

> of common sense is that it is altogether a spiritual thing.
> Nay, common sense is even a celestial thing; common sense
> is not of this world. One can tell the divine origin of com-
> mon sense by this simple test; that it is always crucified.[39]

Common sense has a divine origin. And common sense
is always crucified. But because it has a divine origin, common sense also has a way of coming back to life, as only
divine things can do. We have certainly seen common sense
crucified in our modern world. Are we going to see its
resurrection?

Resurrection is no easy task, first of all because it *does*
involve crucifixion. But also because resurrection means
doing things the opposite way of how they are normally
done. We are accustomed to dead things staying dead. Death
has a certain overwhelming quality to it, which is exactly
why we can become so easily discouraged when we are
constantly fighting the Culture of Death.

When we talk about the Culture of Death, we are not
talking only about abortion and euthanasia—although make
no mistake, we certainly are talking about those things. We
are talking about the culture that has created a mentality
where these things that were once unthinkable are now so
unthinkingly accepted. It came about because of all the
strange little modern philosophies that have worked their
way into our thinking. When G. K. Chesterton honestly
and thoroughly evaluated these philosophies, he realized two
things: that they were wrong, and Christianity was right.
He realized that they were wrong because every one of them,
if taken to its logical conclusion, leads to madness, and then
to self-destruction. It is these things—materialism, relativism, scientific determinism, abstract expressionism, mindless hedonism, rabid socialism, and vapid capitalism—that

[39] *DN*, March 16, 1907.

have all combined to create the Culture of Death. So many things in the modern world have gone wrong: we see art that is disgusting and disturbing, entertainment that glorifies sin, education that is detached from truth and goodness, politics that are filled with corruption and chaos, a commercial system based solely on selfishness, science on steroids, and neighborhoods filled with broken families and lonely people. And that's just the short list.

The question is, do we want to go along with the world, following all its fashions and foolish ideas, or do we want to stand up against it? Do we want to be part of the Culture of Death or the Culture of Life? The easy thing to do is to choose death. The difficult thing to do is to choose life.

The great majority of people know that life is basically a good thing and death is basically a bad thing. This is common sense. Chesterton says that even traffic laws are based on the premise that it is a kindness to people to keep the driver alive.[40] And even though this is completely obvious and should be beyond dispute, yet there are some people who in fact dispute it. They really question whether some people should be kept alive. They are seriously looking for exceptions to the big laws, such as "Thou shalt not kill." Suddenly we find ourselves doing battle with absurdity, trying to defend what is normal, while the abnormal is becoming officially sanctioned: "Whenever we see things done wildly, but taken tamely, then the State is growing insane."[41]

It is a nightmarish battle when the state itself has become insane. Chesterton saw this coming. It would come subtly and slowly because normal people would become passive:

[40] See DN, August 10, 1907.
[41] A Miscellany of Men (Norfolk, Va.: IHS Press, 2004), 47.

> We are no longer in a world in which it is thought normal
> to be moderate or even necessary to be normal. Most men
> now are not so much rushing to extremes as merely sliding
> to extremes; and even reaching the most violent extremes
> by being almost entirely passive.... We can no longer trust
> even the normal man to value and guard his own normality.[42]

It is time for normal men to guard their normality. It is
time to fight for what is right. But we cannot simply condemn what is wrong; we must affirm what is right. That is
the greater and more difficult task. Yes, we must fight the
Culture of Death, but more importantly we must start building a Culture of Life. This is something we cannot merely
talk about. We actually must do it. We actually must live it.
If we do, others will too.

Lesson one? Read Chesterton's novel *Manalive*. Lesson two?
Live it. We can better appreciate the thrill of being alive by
looking at everyday things in a new light or from a different perspective. That is what the main character of the novel
does. To better appreciate his own home, Innocent Smith
breaks into it as a burglar would. To better appreciate his
marriage, he elopes over and over—with the same woman—
who happens to be his wife.

It is a paradox that we can save the world by first saving
ourselves, that is, by gaining a sense of wonder and gratitude that will infect everyone around us. With wonder and
gratitude we can create a Culture of Life. And that is what
Chesterton did. He made it his prayer that God would grant
him the power to stand outside himself in order to see himself better. We can glory in God's creation as we look at
the world around us, but to realize that God made *us*—this
body, these hands, these eyes, this soul—is a profound truth
far more difficult to grasp, a vision far more difficult to see.

[42] *America*, January 4, 1936.

Chesterton's prayer was "Give me eyes to see my eyes."
And he turned this prayer into a poem:

Sunder me from my bones, O sword of God,
Till they stand stark and strange as do the trees;
That I whose heart goes up with the soaring woods
May marvel as much at these.

Sunder me from my blood that in the dark
I hear that red ancestral river run,
Like branching buried floods that find the sea
But never see the sun.

Give me miraculous eyes to see my eyes,
Those rolling mirrors made alive in me,
Terrible crystals more incredible
Than all the things they see.

Sunder me from my soul, that I may see
The sins like streaming wounds, the life's brave beat;
Till I shall save myself, as I would save
A stranger in the street.[43]

[43] "The Sword of Surprise", in *Collected Poetry*, *CW* 10, Part 1:173–74.

15

Abandon Hopelessness,
All Ye Who Enter Here

To make the human family happy is the only possible
object of all education, as of all civilization.

—*The Merry-Go-Round*, June 1924

One of the hardest things to describe in the world is happiness. It seems to come only in momentary bursts, and it
does not hold still long enough for the artist to capture it.
G. K. Chesterton says, "There are twenty minor poets who
can describe fairly impressively an eternity of agony; there
are very few even of the eternal poets who can describe
ten minutes of satisfaction." [1]

With all due respect to those twenty minor poets and
their fairly impressive description of eternal agony, there
really is no excuse for all the effort they have put into the
many books and movies and shows that add to our eternal agony, that do nothing but depress us, that dwell only
on the ugly and the unusual and the unbecoming. Even
most of our comedy has a sad edge to it; the laughter is
hollow. What we almost never see is art that expresses true

[1] *Appreciations and Criticisms of the Works of Charles Dickens*, CW 15:311.

joy. What we almost never hear is laughter that is truly joyful.

Unless, of course, we are reading G. K. Chesterton. He was one of those few eternal poets who could describe not only satisfaction but happiness.

> Happiness is a state of the soul; a state in which our natures are full of the wine of an ancient youth, in which banquets last for ever, and roads lead everywhere, where all things are under the exuberant leadership of faith, hope, and charity.[2]

To be happy is to be in every sense carefree. Chesterton says "it is the happy man who does the useless things."[3] Children of course understand this better than adults. Think of how many useless things a child does throughout the course of a day. And it is precisely during such useless acts when children seem to be most fulfilled. It is when we have them do useful things that their joy suddenly breaks down.

As Chesterton sums it up: earth is a task garden, and heaven is a playground.[4] We are striving to get to heaven, to realize fully and completely the abundant life and eternal joy for which we were made. In the meantime, we do get some glimpses of it, even tastes of it. Joy that is not yet fully realized is called hope.

Chesterton as we have said is a writer of hope and happiness—one of the few. But there is another important writer who hailed from Jolly Old England, who accomplished the same thing. And he was probably the writer who inspired Chesterton more than any other. You've probably heard of him. I'm speaking of Charles Dickens.

---

[2] *Charles Dickens* (1903), *CW* 15:25.
[3] *Orthodoxy*, *CW* 1:221.
[4] See *ILN*, August 17, 1907.

Although their differences are many, there are some easy
and obvious comparisons between these two writers. They
were both incredibly prolific. They both got their start as
journalists—in fact, Charles Dickens was the founder of the
Daily News, the paper where Chesterton later established
himself as a popular essayist. Both were endlessly creative.
What Chesterton said of Dickens is true of himself as well,
that he had "a vitality so vast and so vivid that everything
which it touched came to life".[5] But it was not just creativity for creativity's sake. It was art for the sake of something beyond itself. As Chesterton also said of Dickens, which
is also true of himself: "Dickens was not content with being
original, he had a wild wish to be true."[6]

Charles Dickens was wildly popular in his own time,
but a generation after his death in 1870, he was already
fading from the public memory. Then in 1906, G. K. Chesterton wrote a book that spurred a huge revival of interest
in Dickens. It is still considered the best critical study of
Dickens ever written. It made people appreciate what a
great writer Dickens was, but also what a great writer Chesterton was.

Now, why do you suppose Dickens was fading from the
public memory? It was mostly because scholars did not think
Dickens was important. The colleges and universities, those
institutions whose job it is to *teach*, that is, to pass the great
things of one generation to the next generation, to preserve the culture, to preserve the past, were instead doing
what they do now, mocking tradition and praising innova-
tion, tripping over themselves to be progressive, and rally-
ing the young against the old.

[5] Introduction to *The Pickwick Papers*, Limited Editions Club (Oxford: Oxford
University Press, 1933).
[6] *Charles Dickens* (1906), *CW* 15:148.

But the young have a way of shocking the old, not by being rebellious but by being reactionary. If fathers forget the past, their sons often rise up and remind them about it. And so when the academy fails in its responsibility to serve the young and teach them the time-honored truths, the students then have to teach the teachers.

Though children have much to teach us, there is ironically one thing they cannot teach: hope. Although it is a standard phrase that youth is a time of hope, Chesterton points out that the truth is precisely the opposite. Youth is a time when every disappointment seems like the end of the world. The things that cause a little boy's distress are terrible, not because they are large, but because he doesn't know that they are small.[7]

Hope is a thing that comes with maturity. It is a thing nurtured by tragedy, by a variety of tragedies. Chesterton says, "Hope means hoping when things are hopeless."[8] Jesus says, "Blessed are those who mourn".[9] Saint Paul says that hope is one of the great virtues, along with faith and charity.[10]

But hope is the most subtle of the virtues, the most difficult to understand, certainly the most difficult to explain—perhaps even more difficult to embrace than faith and charity. My friend the actor Kevin O'Brien once said to me: "Hope is the most hated virtue of modern times. It is more despised than chastity. If you don't despair in a cynical hip way, you ain't cool. Think about that. The whole world is conspiring to talk us out of Hope."

Chesterton's book about Charles Dickens is a book about hope. It is a lesson in encouragement.

[7] See ibid., 57.
[8] *Heretics*, *CW* 1:125.
[9] Matthew 5:4.
[10] See 1 Corinthians 13:13.

In the opening chapter, Chesterton offers the reader a most compelling invitation:

> Just as Christianity looked for the honest man inside the thief, democracy looked for the wise man inside the fool. It encouraged the fool to be wise.[11]

> If democracy has disappointed you, do not think of it as a burst bubble, but as a broken heart, an old love-affair. Do not sneer at the time when the creed of humanity was on its honeymoon; treat it with the dreadful reverence that is due to youth. For you, perhaps, a drearier philosophy has covered and eclipsed the earth. The fierce poet of the Middle Ages wrote, "Abandon hope, all ye who enter here," over the gates of the lower world. The emancipated poets of today—which is to say, the minor poets—have written it over the gates of this world. But if we are to understand the story which follows, we must erase that apocalyptic writing, if only for an hour. We must recreate the faith of our fathers, if only as an artistic atmosphere. If, then, you are a pessimist, in reading this story, forego for a little the pleasures of pessimism. Dream for one mad moment that the grass is green. Unlearn that sinister learning that you think so clear; deny that deadly knowledge that you think you know. Surrender the very flower of your culture; give up the very jewel of your pride; abandon hopelessness, all ye who enter here.[12]

When Chesterton became a Catholic, he read in the Church's catechism that the two sins against hope are presumption and despair. This was especially striking to him because he had spent his whole literary life doing battle against presumption and despair, that is, doing battle with

[11] *Charles Dickens, CW* 15:46.
[12] Ibid., 51.

the optimists and the pessimists.[13] Chesterton says that the optimist is the man who thinks everything is good except the pessimist, and the pessimist is the man who thinks everything is bad except himself.[14] We are tempted to associate pessimism with sorrow and optimism with joy. But as Chesterton points out, this is not the case: "Sorrow and pessimism are ... opposite things, since sorrow is founded on the value of something, and pessimism upon the value of nothing."[15]

The corollary is that joy and optimism are opposite things. For joy is founded on the appreciation of something, and optimism on the appreciation of nothing, that is, nothing in particular.

Both sorrow and joy are connected to hope. Sorrow is hope put to the test. Joy is hope fulfilled. Both pessimism and optimism avoid hope. Pessimism regards hope as impossible; optimism regards hope as unnecessary. Pessimism is despair. Optimism is presumption.

We live in a very troubled world. Despair is always knocking on our door. It is always peeking its frightening eyes through our windows. The only weapon against despair is hope. But we also live in a very snide and sneering world. Presumption permeates the airwaves. And the only weapon against presumption is hope.

One of the reasons that Dickens was so popular, that people were so hungry for his words, was that Dickens directly addressed their joys and aspirations.

Dickens did not write what the people wanted. Dickens wanted what the people wanted.[16]

[13] See *Autobiography*, *CW* 16:320–21.
[14] See *Orthodoxy*, *CW* 1:269.
[15] *Charles Dickens*, *CW* 15:60.
[16] Ibid., 99.

> There is a great man who makes every man feel small. But the really great man is the man who makes every man feel great.[17]

How did Dickens do this? He did it with the characters he created. It is truly a wonder when people on a printed page not only spring to life but capture our hearts.

> It is, perhaps, the strongest mark of the divinity of man that he talks of this world as "a strange world," though he has seen no other. We feel that all there is is eccentric, though we do not know what is the centre. This sentiment of the grotesqueness of the universe ran through Dickens's brain and body like the mad blood of the elves. He saw all his streets in fantastic perspectives, he saw all his cockney villas as top heavy and wild, he saw every man's nose twice as big as it was, and every man's eyes like saucers. And this was the basis of his gaiety—the only real basis of any philosophical gaiety. This world is not to be justified as it is justified by the mechanical optimists; it is not to be justified as the best of all possible worlds. Its merit is not that it is orderly and explicable; its merit is that it is wild and utterly unexplained. Its merit is precisely that none of us could have conceived such a thing, that we should have rejected the bare idea of it as miracle and unreason. It is the best of all impossible worlds.[18]

A standard question that we have all been asked is, what book would you want to have with you if you were stranded on a desert island? When most people are asked that question, they either say the Bible or Shakespeare. Chesterton says there's a reason for that. In most cases, it would be the first time that they ever read the Bible or Shakespeare.[19]

[17] Ibid., 43.
[18] Ibid., 203.
[19] See *ILN*, May 23, 1936.

You have probably heard the story of Chesterton's response to this famous question about what book he'd want to have with him on a desert island. He answered, *"Thomas' Guide to Practical Ship-building"*.[20]

But what you probably have not heard is the rest of the story. He went on to say the book he would really like to have on a desert island, to read over and over again, was *The Pickwick Papers* by Charles Dickens.[21]

He considers *Pickwick* to be Dickens' best book, but not his best novel.[22] It can hardly be called a novel. It has no discernable plot. The story, if it is a story and not rather a hundred stories, is made out of a hundred or a thousand other things and people. It is made out of the things and people that the travelers pick up as they go along. Everything is lightly tossed to other people, to people merely passing in the crowd. The best things that the hero finds are never the things he is looking for. The unimportant characters are the important characters.[23]

Those are all good reasons for liking the book, but there is one other reason why Chesterton liked *Pickwick Papers* so much. When we are reading a good book, we do not want it to end. Well, for Chesterton, *Pickwick* is the perfect book because it really does not end. On the final page, Mr. Pickwick and Sam Weller's adventures have just begun, and we can imagine that they are still going on. And as a way of reflecting that perfection, Chesterton ends his own book on Dickens in the same way, not with a conclusion, but with a doorway to eternity.

---

[20] Cyril Clemens, *Chesterton as Seen by His Contemporaries* (New York: Gordon Press, 1972), 131.

[21] See ibid.

[22] That honor he gave to *Bleak House*. See *Appreciations*, *CW* 15:342.

[23] See the Introduction to *The Pickwick Papers*.

We shall not be much further troubled with the little artists who found Dickens too sane for their sorrows and too clean for their delights. But we have a long way to travel before we get back to what Dickens meant: and the passage is along a rambling English road, a twisting road such as Mr. Pickwick travelled. But this at least is part of what he meant; that comradeship and serious joy are not interludes in our travel; but that rather our travels are interludes in comradeship and joy, which through God shall endure for ever. The inn does not point to the road; the road points to the inn. And all roads point at last to an ultimate inn, where we shall meet Dickens and all his characters: and when we drink again it shall be from the great flagons in the tavern at the end of the world.[24]

Even though that would be a perfect way to end this chapter, I am going to keep going. Perhaps this will be the chapter that never ends.

Although *Pickwick* was Chesterton's favorite work by Dickens, the hands-down favorite in our day is the short story "A Christmas Carol". We have all seen many versions of it. Why is it so appealing? Because it is a story about conversion, a story that mocks the miser who thinks the surplus population would do well to die, which is a prophecy of the modern mentality that hates life itself. But this story shows that there is hope even for a hopeless character like Scrooge.

Conversion is not just about starting over, starting new. Conversion is about turning—turning back, embracing not the new but the old, the tradition.

Chesterton praised Dickens for saving Christmas in England, for defending a tradition that was being lost. Christmas really was in danger of being done away with in those countries where Protestantism and Puritanism had taken over.

---

[24] *Charles Dickens*, *CW* 15:208–9.

In fighting for Christmas, Dickens was fighting for the old European festival, Pagan and Christian, for that trinity of eating, drinking and praying which to moderns appears irreverent, for the holy day which is really a holiday.[25]

It is interesting that Dickens' "A Christmas Carol" continues to be a perennial favorite in a culture where Christmas is still under attack. It is an important work, not just because it is about saving Christmas, but because it is about tradition, and we are in serious danger of having all of our great traditions swept away by the cult of progress. With the emphasis on everything being new and improved, and our desire to get new things, this breathless keeping up, this terror of being left behind, we are doing everything exactly backwards, exactly wrong. We do not realize that the most important thing is not about getting what is new but about not losing what is old. The most important people in our time will be those who protect the past. They will be most appreciated in the future.

Dickens preserved the past. Chesterton preserved Dickens. And now there are a happy few who are working to preserve Chesterton. We recognize the same greatness in Chesterton that he recognized in Dickens, one not only who used his literary gifts to bring good cheer and foster the neglected virtue of hope, but who fought for truth and for justice. And he inspires us to do the same. He defends local things, which makes us want to defend local things, even if they are not the same local things that Chesterton defended. One of the worst trends at present in America is the centralization of everything and the loss of local things. There is a sameness that is steadily creeping over the whole country, the same ribbons of concrete crawling with the same automobiles, the same giant chain stores selling the

[25] Ibid., 131.

same stuff, the same loudspeakers blaring the same music, the same movies with the same plots, the same suburbs with the same houses, the same sins with the same excuses. Those are things we feel we must fight. It is only in defending the local things that we defend the universal things: the family, the fellowship of friends, and the faith. Chesterton says we do not need a Church that is moved by the world, but a Church that will move the world.[26] That is why G. K. Chesterton is such an important ally. He never wearies of telling the truth, which is why we never weary of quoting him. The truth is always fresh and exciting.

> The man who has found a truth dances about like a boy who has found a shilling; he breaks into extravagances, as the Christian churches broke into gargoyles. In one sense truth alone can be exaggerated; nothing else can stand the strain.[27]

Chesterton's timelessness and universality are epitomized in his book on Charles Dickens, a book that is supposedly a work of literary criticism. In it he writes, "Every train of thought may end in ecstasy, and all roads lead to Elfland."[28] That is an idea that is full of hope. Two years after he wrote this book, Chesterton penned one of his greatest masterpieces, *Orthodoxy*. The centerpiece of that book is a chapter called "The Ethics of Elfland", in which Chesterton allows us to see that the universal truths found in fairy tales point directly to Christianity. Elfland was for Chesterton the road to Christianity—a road that took him all the way to Rome. All roads lead to Rome—through Elfland. It is

[26] See Maisie Ward, *Return to Chesterton* (New York: Sheed and Ward, 1952), 468.
[27] *Charles Dickens*, CW 15:145.
[28] Ibid., 49.

interesting that Dickens, who was not a Catholic, helped point Chesterton to the Catholic Church.

> Dickens is ... close to popular religion, which is the ultimate and reliable religion. He conceives an endless joy. ... He has not come, as a writer, that his creatures may copy life and copy its narrowness; he has come that they may have life, and that they may have it more abundantly. It is absurd indeed that Christians should be called the enemies of life because they wish life to last for ever; it is more absurd still to call the old comic writers dull because they wished their unchanging characters to last for ever. Both popular religion, with its endless joys, and the old comic story, with its endless jokes, have in our time faded together. We are too weak to desire that undying vigour. We believe that you can have too much of a good thing—a blasphemous belief, which at one blow wrecks all the heavens that men have hoped for.[29]

I know of several people who would never willingly have picked up a book by G. K. Chesterton because they were certain to dislike him based on any number of preconceptions. But, quite by accident, they have picked up a book of literary criticism on Charles Dickens, only to discover too late that it was written by Chesterton. Too late, because they have wandered in too far and cannot escape. It is not that they have finally discovered Dickens. It is not that they have finally discovered Chesterton. It is that they have at last discovered the most underrated virtue: hope.

[29] Ibid., 89.

16

To Be

Hamlet pretended to be mad in order to deceive fools.
We cannot complain if he has succeeded.

—*Illustrated London News*, September 14, 1929

As a literary critic, G. K. Chesterton is less a critic of literature than he is a critic of the critics. This is especially true when it comes to critics of Shakespeare.

Chesterton is a critic of those who would psychoanalyze not only Shakespeare but Shakespeare's characters, of those who would try to force and squeeze Shakespeare into narrow modern philosophies, of those who concluded that Shakespeare was despairing (only because Shakespeare could express their own despair), of those who would turn "good poetry into bad metaphysics",[1] of those who cannot connect with the audience and who therefore cannot understand why Shakespeare *does* connect with the audience (and why after four centuries he can still pull them in), of those who have the audacity to say how they would have written Shakespeare (when it is Shakespeare who "has written us"[2]).

[1] *The Speaker*, May 11, 1901.
[2] *DN*, January 2, 1907.

He was also a critic of those critics who are simply small—
like those who complain that Shakespeare borrowed all his
plots. Chesterton says, "[I]f Shakespeare borrowed, he jolly
well paid back." [3]

Finally, he is a critic of those who say Shakespeare did
not write Shakespeare.

Most critics suffer from what Chesterton calls "the art of
missing the point". They are so intent on finding the things
that are not there, that they miss the things that are. The
function of the critic is to explain to the audience what it
does feel, not what it *should* feel.

Chesterton shares with Shakespeare at least one great artistic strength: the ability to connect with the audience. They
share the basic artistic instincts of the audience, the desire
for beauty, for joy, for justice, and for a joke. They are
not at war with the audience as are so many modern
artists. Chesterton's argument is that the misunderstood artist is misunderstood because, well, he is not a very good
artist.

> The artistic temperament is a disease that afflicts amateurs.
> It is a disease which arises from men not having sufficient
> power of expression to utter and get rid of the element of
> art in their being. It is healthful to every sane man to utter
> the art within him; it is essential to every sane man to get
> rid of the art within him at all costs.
>
> Artists of a large and wholesome vitality get rid of their
> art easily, as they breathe easily, or perspire easily. But in
> artists of less force, the thing becomes a pressure, and pro-
> duces a definite pain, which is called the artistic tempera-
> ment. Thus, very great artists are able to be ordinary men—
> men like Shakespeare or Browning. There are many real
> tragedies of the artistic temperament, tragedies of vanity or

[3] *Chaucer, CW* 18:156.

violence or fear. But the great tragedy of the artistic temperament is that it cannot produce any art.[4]

The greatness of an artist is measured by his ability to express
the inexpressible. What Shakespeare and Chesterton and any
great poet does is express what we already know but cannot express. We recognize it to be true immediately, and
we wish that we could have said it so well ourselves. They
have the common touch and the uncommon touch, the
ability to combine the ordinary with the extraordinary. It is
why Shakespeare and Chesterton share another quality: they
are both easily quotable.

But this has actually created a big problem—and a small
irony. Shakespeare's great achievement has been weakened
by what Chesterton calls "the abominable habit of quoting
Shakespeare without reading Shakespeare".[5]

There is an old joke about the woman who saw the play
Hamlet and complained that it was nothing but quotations.
And there are people who read Chesterton's book *Orthodoxy* and, quite understandably, underline almost every sentence, but then have a hard time explaining what the book
is about.

There is a danger in those really good lines. As Chesterton says of Shakespeare's great quotations, "They have a
mysterious power of making the world weary of a few fixed
and disconnected words, and yet leaving the world entirely
ignorant of the real meaning of those words."[6]

And so, we have to start by stating the obvious truth that
there is more to Shakespeare than his great quotations. And
there is more to G. K. Chesterton than his great quotations.

---

[4] *Heretics, CW* 1:171.
[5] *The Spice of Life and Other Essays*, ed. Dorothy Collins (Beaconsfield,
Eng.: Darwen Finlayson, 1964), 53.
[6] Ibid., 54.

However, it is impossible to talk about either one without
quoting them. It is also foolish, because they are, together,
the most intensely quotable writers in the English language. And that is why it is such a pleasure to put the two
together, to watch one great writer writing about another.

One of the first things that Chesterton says about Shakespeare is that he was a mystic, that "he saw in every stone
in the street things which cannot be uttered till the end of
the world." [7] Now to say that Shakespeare was a mystic
raises the very interesting question, what was Shakespeare's
religion? How does Chesterton deal with that question?

Nearly all Englishmen are either Shakespearians or Milto-
nians. I do not mean that they admire one more than the
other; because everyone in his senses must admire both of
them infinitely. I mean that each represents something in
the make-up of England; and that the two things are so far
antagonistic that it is really impossible not to be secretly on
one side or the other. The difference, in so far as it concerns the two men, can be expressed in all sorts of ways;
but every way taken by itself is inadequate. Shakespeare represents the Catholic, Milton the Protestant.... Shakespeare
never went to an English University; Milton did. Milton
regarded the trick of rhyming with contempt; Shakespeare
used it even in the most inappropriate moments. Milton
had no humour; Shakespeare had very much too much....
Milton was probably unkind to his wife; Shakespeare's wife
was probably unkind to him. Milton started from the very
first with a clear idea of making poetry. Shakespeare started
with a very vague idea of somehow making money. Whenever Milton speaks of religion, it is Milton's religion: the
religion that Milton has made. Whenever Shakespeare speaks
of religion (which is only seldom), it is of a religion that
has made him. Lastly, Milton was mostly blind, and took

great care of his manuscripts; while Shakespeare was often blind drunk and took no care of his.[8]

Some of Chesterton's most important points are made as offhand remarks or asides. Here, as part of a comparison between Shakespeare and Milton, he just tosses it off that Shakespeare was Catholic. Now that is a major statement, but for Chesterton it is a matter-of-fact statement. If Shakespeare was a Catholic, it sheds an entirely different light on his plays than if he were writing as someone who had rejected the Catholic Church. It also means he was not merely a Catholic but an illegal Catholic. For under Queen Elizabeth I the Catholic Church was suppressed, and many English Catholics died for their faith. And so when Chesterton made the remark that Shakespeare was Catholic, many people immediately took him to task for it, and as with anything, Chesterton was only too happy to discuss it. He admitted that it is difficult to explain how you can tell that someone is of a particular religion when they have not stated it overtly. You are basing it on an impression, but since religion has to do with everything, then you are talking about an impression of everything, and everything is always a difficult subject to discuss in a fifteen-hundred-word newspaper column. But "everything" is the subject that Chesterton always writes about.

And so Chesterton happily defends his claim that Shakespeare was Catholic:

> Shakespeare is possessed through and through with the feeling which is the first and finest idea of Catholicism: that truth exists whether we like it or not, and that it is for us to accommodate ourselves to it. [When Milton writes of truth, it is to] justify the ways of God to men. But when

[8] *ILN*, May 18, 1907.

Shakespeare speaks of the divine truth, it is always as something from which he himself may have fallen away, something that he himself may have forgotten. ... I really do not
know how this indescribable matter can be better described
than by simply saying this; that Milton's religion was Milton's religion, and that Shakespeare's religion was not
Shakespeare's.[9]

Though Chesterton is defending the idea that Shakespeare was a Catholic, these lines were written when Chesterton himself was not a Catholic. But after his conversion,
he wrote a book on Chaucer, and in that book he also
makes reference to Shakespeare, and to Shakespeare's Cathol-
icism. He says the idea that Shakespeare was a Catholic "is
a thing that every Catholic feels by every sort of conver-
gent common sense to be true. It is supported by the few
external and political facts we know; it is utterly unmistak-
able in the general spirit and atmosphere"[10] of Shakespeare's writings. This is particularly true of the play *Hamlet*.

Consider the idea that *Hamlet* is a Catholic play, that it
represents the dilemma of English Catholics when their
Church and their faith was unjustly and murderously stolen
from them and that the only way to get it back is to, well,
murder the monarch. There is a certain gravity to the
situation.

Hamlet is not only a huge figure in Shakespeare's play;
he is, says Chesterton, a huge figure in all of literature. We
have never fully appreciated his dilemma, his motivation,
his hesitancy, his actions, and his remorse. He is bigger than
any denunciations of him and even bigger than any defenses
of him. But in the early twentieth century, Hamlet was made
very small by the new science of psychology. Hamlet was a

[9] *ILN*, June 8, 1907.
[10] *Chaucer, CW* 18:333.

favorite subject of Freud. The leading Freudian idea was that we suffer from the suppression of our impulses. Chesterton points out, however, that Shakespeare's plays make precisely the opposite point.[11] It is only after these characters have given into their impulses that they really begin to suffer. Lady Macbeth starts sleep walking, not because she resisted an impulse to murder Duncan, but because she yielded to it. Hamlet's uncle is tortured by the fact that he gave into the temptation to murder his brother and marry his sister-in-law. Macbeth is haunted by Banquo's ghost instead of by all the living souls of the people whom he wanted to murder but did not.

One group of modern critics, borrowing from the psychoanalysts, claim there is some subconscious revulsion in Hamlet. But as Chesterton points out, the subconscious revulsion is in the modern critic. It is the critic who is trying to avoid something. He is avoiding the morality in which Shakespeare believed. Hamlet's struggle is between duty and inclination. The critic tries to make it a struggle between consciousness and subconsciousness. "He gives Hamlet a complex to avoid giving him a conscience."[12] But the whole concept of tragedy is based on morality. It means doing the right thing, even if we detest doing it. We may risk death doing the right thing. We risk something worse by failing to do the right thing.

Another idea that the critics get wrong about Hamlet is that they call him a skeptic.

If Hamlet had been at all a sceptic there would have been no tragedy of Hamlet. If he had had any scepticism to exercise, he could have exercised it at once upon the highly improbable ghost of his father. He could have called that

[11] See *Fancies Versus Fads* (London: Methuen, 1923), 25.
[12] Ibid., 30.

eloquent person a hallucination, have married Ophelia, and
gone on eating bread and butter.[13]

Chesterton says that the mistake of regarding Hamlet as
a skeptic arose out of quoting stilted passages out of their
context, such as "To be or not to be",[14] or (much worse)
the passage in which he says with an almost obvious ges-
ture of fatigue, "Why then, 'tis none to you; for there is
nothing either good or bad, but thinking makes it so".[15]
Hamlet says this because he is getting exceedingly irritated
by having to hang around with Rosencrantz and Guilden-
stern. But if you listen to the rest of the speech, it is very
clear that these are not the words of a skeptic:

> This goodly frame, the earth, seems to me a sterile prom-
> ontory;
> this most excellent canopy the air, look you,
> this brave o'erhanging firmament,
> this majestical roof fretted with golden fire—
> why it appeareth no other thing to me than a foul and
> pestilent congregation of vapours.
> What a piece of work is man! How noble in reason! how
> infinite in faculty! in form and moving, how express and
> admirable!
> in action how like an angel!
> in apprehension how like a god! the beauty of the world!
> the paragon of animals!
> And yet, to me, what is this quintessence of dust?[16]

[13] *Lunacy and Letters* (London: Sheed and Ward, 1958), 121.
[14] William Shakespeare, *Hamlet*, Ignatius Critical Editions (San Francisco:
Ignatius Press, 2008), 3.1.56. References are to act, scene, and line.
[15] Ibid., 2.2.248–50.
[16] Ibid., 2.2.292–309.

That is not a pessimistic passage even though some people claim it is. It is, says Chesterton, "perhaps the most optimistic passage in all human literature." [17]

> It is the absolute expression of the ultimate fact of the faith of Hamlet; his faith that, although he cannot see the world is good, yet certainly it is good; his faith that, though he cannot see man as the image of God, yet certainly he is the image of God. The modern ... conception of Hamlet, believes only in mood. But the real Hamlet, like the Catholic Church, believes in reason. Many fine optimists have praised man when they felt like praising him. Only Hamlet has praised man when he felt like kicking him.... Many poets ... have been optimistic when they felt optimistic. Only Shakespeare has been optimistic when he felt pessimistic. This is the definition of a faith. A faith is that which is able to survive a mood. [18]

Hamlet knew that there was a truth beyond himself; he even knew that he might be wrong, which is only another way of stating that there is something that is right. "The real sceptic never thinks he is wrong; for the real sceptic does not think that there is any wrong. He sinks through floor after floor of a bottomless universe." [19]

As great as the play *Hamlet* is, Chesterton claims that *Macbeth* is actually Shakespeare's greatest drama and greatest tragedy.

Just as Hamlet is accused of being a skeptic and a pessimist based on few often-quoted passages, Shakespeare is accused of being a pessimist because of *Macbeth*. One of the accusers was George Bernard Shaw, who pointed to the "out brief candle" soliloquy.

[17] *Lunacy and Letters*, 122.
[18] Ibid.
[19] Ibid., 123.

To-morrow, and to-morrow, and to-morrow,
Creeps in this petty pace from day to day
To the last syllable of recorded time,
And all our yesterdays have lights fools
The way to dusty death. Out, out, brief candle!
Life's but a walking shadow, a poor player,
That struts and frets his hour upon the stage,
And then is heard no more; it is a tale
Told by an idiot, full of sound and fury,
Signifying nothing.[20]

As Chesterton explains to Shaw, the importance of this speech is in its dramatic value, not its philosophic value. It is Macbeth at his lowest point, just before his final defeat. "It is a speech", says Chesterton, "made by a wicked and wasted human soul confronted by his own colossal failure." It is not a metaphysical statement at all; it is an emotional outburst. To call Shakespeare a pessimist for having written the words "out, out, brief candle" is the same as calling him a champion of the ideal of celibacy for having written the words "Get thee to the nunnery." "It is not Shakespeare's fault," says Chesterton, "that, having to write pessimism for the purpose of a theatrical point, he happened to write much better pessimism than the people who are silly enough to be pessimists." [21]

I think the greatest drama in the world is "Macbeth" ... because it is the one Christian drama. . . . I mean by Christian [its] strong sense of spiritual liberty and of sin; the idea that the best man can be as bad as he chooses. You may call Othello a victim of chance. You may call Hamlet a victim

[20] William Shakespeare, *Macbeth*, Ignatius Critical Editions (San Francisco: Ignatius Press, 2010), 5.5.19–20. References are to act, scene, and line.
[21] *DN*, April 29, 1905.

of temperament. You cannot call Macbeth anything but a
victim of Macbeth.[22]

Macbeth is the supreme Christian tragedy, as opposed to
Oedipus, which is the supreme pagan tragedy. "It is the whole
point about Oedipus that he does not know what he is
doing. And it is the whole point about Macbeth that he
does know what he is doing. It is not a tragedy of Fate but
a tragedy of Freewill." [23]

When Chesterton says it is the tragedy of free will, he
means there comes a moment in the play where—if it is
acted properly, when Macbeth says suddenly, "We will
proceed no further in this business"—you really believe
that the play could end differently! And you hope that it
will, you hope that Macbeth won't murder Duncan. But
he does.

The main lesson we get from Macbeth is that you cannot commit a sin to become happy. "You cannot do a mad
thing in order to reach sanity."

> The crime does not get rid of the problem. Its effect is so
> bewildering that one may say that the crime does not get
> rid of the temptation. Make a morbid decision and you
> will only become more morbid; do a lawless thing and
> you will only get into an atmosphere much more suffo-
> cating than that of law. Indeed, it is a mistake to speak of
> a man as "breaking out." The lawless man never breaks
> out; he breaks in. He smashes a door and finds himself in
> another room, he smashes a wall and finds himself in a yet
> smaller one. The more he shatters the more his habitation
> shrinks. Where he ends you may read in the end of
> *Macbeth*.[24]

[22] *ILN*, March 16, 1912.
[23] *ILN*, September 14, 1929.
[24] *Spice of Life*, 45.

The other great thing about the play *Macbeth*, the element that compounds the tragedy, is the character of Lady Macbeth: the loyal wife who wants what is best for her man. Chesterton says that the most masculine kind of man always is ruled by his wife. In fact, Chesterton is always suspicious of the man who is not just a little afraid of his wife. Thus, unlike most married couples in fiction, you can believe that Mr. and Mrs. Macbeth are actually married.

> The dispute that goes on between Macbeth and his wife about the murder of Duncan is almost word for word a dispute which goes on at any suburban breakfast-table about something else. It is merely a matter of changing "Infirm of purpose, give me the daggers", into "infirm of purpose, give me the postage stamps".... The strengths of the two partners differ in kind. The woman has more of that strength on the spot which is called industry. The man has more of that strength in reserve which is called laziness.[25]

Even though Chesterton maintains that *Macbeth* is Shakespeare's greatest drama, he does not say it is his greatest play. That honor he gives to *A Midsummer Night's Dream*.

> The sentiment of the play can be summed up in one sentence. It is the mysticism of happiness. That is to say, it is the conception that as man lives upon a borderland he may find himself in the spiritual or supernatural atmosphere, not only through being profoundly sad or meditative, but by being extravagantly happy. The soul might be rapt out of the body in an agony of sorrow, or a trance of ecstasy; but it might also be rapt out of the body in a paroxysm of laughter. Sorrow we know can go beyond itself; so, according to Shakespeare, can pleasure go beyond itself and become

[25] Ibid., 52.

something dangerous and unknown.... In pure poetry and the intoxication of words, Shakespeare never rose higher than he rises in this play.[26]

So Shakespeare wrote all these amazing plays, but for some reason the question is still asked, "Who wrote Shakespeare?"

Chesterton answers, "Shakespeare is quite himself; it is only some of his critics who have discovered that he was somebody else." [27]

During Chesterton's time the leading naysayers claimed that Francis Bacon wrote Shakespeare, as opposed to a slightly later time when they claimed that Christopher Marlowe wrote Shakespeare, and now our time when most of them claim that the Earl of Oxford wrote Shakespeare. These theories have something in common: they all originate in America.

> The great Transatlantic theory that Shakespeare was not Shakespeare, but someone else with a different name, is one of those intellectual pestilences which break out recurrently in countries that do not pay sufficient attention to intellectual sanitation.[28]

The argument about who really wrote Shakespeare always has as its basis the suspicion that a mere actor, not educated in the great English universities, could not possibly have penned such masterpieces, which is the argument of the snob.

But then there is another argument raised: "Why", it is asked, "was there not more excitement about such a

---

[26] *The Common Man* (New York: Sheed and Ward, 1950), 12–13.
[27] *Orthodoxy, CW* 1:219.
[28] *DN*, May 6, 1901.

sensational genius?" To which, says Chesterton, the obvious answer is, "Why indeed?"[29]

Which brings me to my final point. You see, I maintain that G. K. Chesterton is the greatest English writer of the twentieth century. And the objection to that claim is usually something like "If he's so great, why haven't more people heard of him? Why isn't he taught in all the universities and colleges? Why is there not more excitement about such a sensational genius?" To which the obvious answer is: "Why, indeed?"

[29] *ILN*, October 22, 1921.

17

The Exception Proves the Rule

Men cannot even enjoy riot when the riot has become
the rule. The world ... has come ... to boasting of being
lawless; but there is no fun in it, because lawlessness is
the law.

—"The Unpsychological Age", *Sidelights*

G. K. Chesterton has a gift for generalization, just as he has
a gift for paradox. However, there are many people who
dislike generalization even more than they dislike paradox.
Their typical reaction to a generalization is to contradict it
with some bizarre example. If we say, "Wearing a seat belt
while driving can save your life if you get into an accident", they might respond, "But what if a forty-five-ton
truck is about to tip over on your car and you need to get
out quickly?" or, "But I have a bladder condition, and the
force of a sudden stop while I'm strapped in could aggra-
vate it, perhaps fatally." They think their stunning exception has disproved our point. But actually they have proved
it because the exception proves the rule.

The exception proves the rule. What does that mean
exactly? I must confess I never knew what it meant—until
Chesterton explained it for me. It is a very important

concept. In fact, Chesterton says that a "silent anarchy is eating out our society" and it is all because we have "an incapacity to grasp that the exception proves the rule." *Exceptio probat regulam* is an ancient and classical dictum. It means, says Chesterton, "if you treat a peculiar thing in a peculiar way, you thereby imply that ordinary things are not to be treated in that way.... Anything in a special situation shows, by implication, that all things are not in that situation." [1] So, to take a vacation is something special, which implies that most of the time you have to work. To say that a madman is irresponsible implies that a normal man is responsible. To go to the doctor when you are ill implies that you do not need a doctor when you are well.

> A wall is like a rule; and the gates are like the exceptions that prove the rule. The man making it has to decide where his rule will run and where his exceptions shall stand. He cannot have a city that is all gates any more than a house that is all windows; nor is it possible to have a law that consists entirely of liberties. [2]

It is interesting that whenever we state what the Church's rules are, people immediately want to talk about the exceptions. They think they can somehow trip us up this way, as if the exception *dis*proves the rule instead of proving it.

For instance, when a married man is ordained as a Roman Catholic priest it is always in the news. That is partly because the news is nothing but exceptions. The news never reports the number of people who have not been robbed or not been murdered or who have successfully driven their car from one point to another without loss of life or limb. The married Catholic priest is news because normally priests

---

[1] *ILN*, February 1, 1913.
[2] *The New Jerusalem, CW* 20:229.

are celibate. The Church has a rule about celibacy, but it makes certain rare exceptions, for instance, for converts who have previously been clergymen or for those who are ordained under an Eastern rite of the Catholic Church. There is a reason for the rule, and a reason for the exception. The exception has not overruled the rule: the rule is still in place and still the norm. Celibacy is not only the rule but the ideal, and you will find, though it may come as a surprise, that married priests (and especially their wives) affirm the wisdom of this rule.

When we teach the Church's very strong and clear stance on abortion, people will immediately object: "But what about cases of rape or incest?" They think they have somehow won the argument with this, when in fact they have lost it. They have with their statement conceded that abortion is normally wrong. By wanting to talk about what they think is an exception, they are admitting the rule. But in this case, the Church does not even concede the exception. Rape and incest are indeed exceptional, that is, they are not the normal circumstances under which a woman becomes pregnant. They are tragic, which means heartbreaking, but they do not provide a license to kill babies. Even though one kind of innocence has been defiled in the act of conception, it is not properly dealt with by destroying another kind of innocence. Sometimes defending life means defending suffering. Sometimes defending the Church's teaching means defending suffering, because the Church defends sacrifice, from the sacrificial love of a parent for a child, to the sacrificial love of one person laying down his life for another, as epitomized by Christ, who laid himself down for the whole world.

Sometimes we allow the exceptions; sometimes we do not allow the exceptions. In either case, we recognize that the exceptions are exceptions. They are not the rule. But

the world does not understand that exceptions are exceptions because it does not understand that rules are rules. By
focusing only on the abnormal, the world has lost sight of
the normal. The ordinary truths are no longer defended
because they are not even defined. As a result, we live in a
society where some of the most important and essential rules
are not so much disobeyed as neglected and even forgotten,
and we try to operate under a welter of exceptions. "The
exception has become the rule, and that is the worst of all
possible tyrannies."[3] Nearly a century after Chesterton
uttered this prophetic observation, a certain Catholic car-
dinal stood up before the whole world and said that we are
living under the dictatorship of relativism. A few days later,
he was elected Pope Benedict XVI. His statement mirrors
Chesterton's exactly. Relativism is nothing other than the
exception becoming the rule. When lawlessness becomes
the law, it is tyranny. The tyrant makes his own truth. So
does the relativist. They are not persuaded by arguments
from a universal truth or by common sense. They answer as
Professor Lucifer answers the monk Michael in the opening chapter of Chesterton's novel *The Ball and the Cross*.

Lucifer and Michael. Even the dimmer literary critics
among us are able to catch the symbolism in the names of
these two characters, who are having a rather remarkable
debate while floating over London in a flying ship. The
imaginative scene has the ship nearly bumping into, well,
the title of the novel, the ball, on top of which stands a
cross, which together stand atop the dome of St. Paul's
Cathedral.

"I was telling you just now, Michael, that I can prove the
best part of the rationalist case and the Christian humbug

[3] *ILN*, November 21, 1914.

from any symbol you liked to give me, from any instance I came across. Here is an instance with a vengeance. What could possibly express your philosophy and my philosophy better than the shape of that cross and the shape of this ball? This globe is reasonable; that cross is unreasonable. It is a four-legged animal, with one leg longer than the others. The globe is inevitable. The cross is arbitrary. Above all the globe is at unity with itself; the cross is primarily and above all things at enmity with itself. The cross is the conflict of two hostile lines, of irreconcilable direction. That silent thing up there is essentially a collision, a crash, a struggle in stone. Pah! that sacred symbol of yours has actually given its name to a description of desperation and muddle. When we speak of men at once ignorant of each other and frustrated by each other, we say they are at cross-purposes. Away with the thing! The very shape of it is a contradiction in terms."

"What you say is perfectly true," said Michael, with serenity. "But we like contradictions in terms. Man is a contradiction in terms; he is a beast whose superiority to other beasts consists in having fallen. That cross is, as you say, an eternal collision; so am I. That is a struggle in stone. Every form of life is a struggle in flesh. The shape of the cross is irrational, just as the shape of the human animal is irrational. You say the cross is a quadruped with one limb longer than the rest. I say man is a quadruped who only uses two of his legs."

The Professor frowned thoughtfully for an instant, and said: "Of course everything is relative, and I would not deny that the element of struggle and self-contradiction, represented by that cross, has a necessary place at a certain evolutionary stage. But surely the cross is the lower development and the sphere the higher. After all it is easy enough to see what is really wrong with Wren's architectural arrangement."

"And what is that, pray?" inquired Michael, meekly.

"The cross is on top of the ball," said Professor Lucifer, simply. "That is surely wrong. The ball should be on top of the cross. The cross is a mere barbaric prop; the ball is perfection. The cross at its best is but the bitter tree of man's history; the ball is the rounded, the ripe and final fruit. And the fruit should be at the top of the tree, not at the bottom of it."

"Oh!" said the monk, a wrinkle coming into his forehead, "so you think that in a rationalistic scheme of symbolism the ball should be on top of the cross?"

"It sums up my whole allegory," said the professor.

"Well, that is really very interesting," resumed Michael slowly, "because I think in that case you would see a most singular effect, an effect that has generally been achieved by all those able and powerful systems which rationalism, or the religion of the ball, has produced to lead or teach mankind. You would see, I think, that thing happen which is always the ultimate embodiment and logical outcome of your logical scheme."

"What are you talking about?" asked Lucifer. "What would happen?"

"I mean it would fall down," said the monk, looking wistfully into the void.[4]

In the entertaining and inventive debate about the meaning of the symbols, the ball that represents atheistic rationalism and the cross that represents Christianity, we might have missed a very telling comment from Professor Lucifer. He says, "Everything is relative."

Chesterton prophetically puts this modern argument in the mouth of the devil in a novel over a century ago, well before relativism would run wild in today's world.

[4] *The Ball and the Cross*, CW 7:41–43.

How did we get to the point where we have lost our ability to appeal to unchanging and absolute truths? First of all, there is the problem that we are fallen creatures. Secondly, there is the problem that we continue to fall—that is, we fall for fashionable ideas. We especially fall for fashionable ideas when they come couched in scientific jargon.

In the early twentieth century, a new scientific theory took the world by storm: the theory of relativity. Classical physics was suddenly challenged by Einstein's theories of curved space and warped time, prompting Chesterton to announce: "Einstein has appeared; and even gravity has begun to behave with levity." [5]

The amazing thing was that almost no one could explain Einstein's ideas, yet nearly everyone assumed he was correct. Chesterton notes at the time that there was a "social flutter" at the very mention of Einstein's name. What it demonstrated was not that people's thinking had expanded, but that they had stopped thinking for themselves. Einstein became a catchword, a substitute for thinking.

It was startling that Einstein should become so famous even while his ideas remained obscure, but stranger still was that the theory of relativity should pave the way to the philosophy of relativism. A scientific theory that almost no one understood was being used to undermine religious ideas that almost everyone understood.

But Einstein's theory did not attack religion; what it attacked was science. If it attacked any philosophy, it was the philosophy of materialism.

> Science was supposed to bully us into being rationalists; but it is now supposed to be bullying us into being irrationalists. The science of Einstein might rather be called following our unreason as far as it will go, seeing whether the

brain will crack under the conception that space is curved, or that parallel straight lines always meet.[6]

No mystic of any mystical school would ever have swept away matter and materialism so ruthlessly as the physicists have done. There was not a parson in all the parishes of the world who would have rebelled against the laws of Newton, left to himself; or desired to dispute with the discoverer of the Differential Calculus. It is a scientist and a sceptic who offers to prove that Newton is nonsense; or, perhaps, rather to prove that the nonsense of Einstein is more true than the sense of Newton. I am not prepared for a moment to arbitrate between the paradoxes of the new astronomy and the rationalism of the old. I only say that the attack on astronomy has come from astronomers, not from astrologers or flat-earthers or adherents of really antiquated superstitions; still less from sane and normal and traditional Christians.[7]

While the foundations of physics may have been shaken by Einstein's theory, the theory of relativity represents no threat to Christianity. As Chesterton points out, the Athanasian Creed does not say that parallel straight lines never meet, so it is unaffected by anything Einstein might say about them.[8] But when people move from physics to metaphysics, still talking about universal relativity, claiming that everything is as relative as everything else, relative to nobody knows what, they are, as Chesterton says, "simply knocking the bottom out of the world and the human brain, and leaving a bottomless abyss of bosh."[9]

People may wish they could understand Einstein; Chesterton wishes they would understand understanding. The purpose of knowing anything is to lead us to an ultimate

[6] *The New Jerusalem*, CW 20:328.
[7] *ILN*, May 9, 1931.
[8] See *ILN*, August 21, 1920.
[9] *ILN*, August 31, 1935.

truth. "The deepest of all desires for knowledge is the desire to know what the world is for and what we are for." [10] If we begin by thinking that truth is relative or changeable or flexible or foggy, we will conclude that truth is trivial. If we let scientific theories determine or sway our theology, we are falling for a fallacy. We are falling into that "bottomless abyss of bosh". It is ironic, even laughable, that people will immediately and unthinkingly accept the authority of Einstein or some other scientific expert, or any so-called expert, but they will not accept the authority of the pope, who certainly has more credentials than most of the other experts.

Ultimately, it is science that is trivial; it is theology that needs to be taken a lot more seriously.

> For some mad reason in this mad world of ours the things about which men differ most are exactly the things about which they must be got to agree. Men can agree on the fact that the earth goes round the sun. But then it does not matter a dump whether the earth goes round the sun or the Pleiades. But men cannot agree about morals; sex, property, individual rights, fixity of contracts, patriotism, suicide, public habits of health—these are exactly the things that men tend to fight about. And these are exactly the things that they must not fight about. These are exactly the things that must be settled somehow, and settled on strict principles. Study each of them, and you will find each of them works back certainly to a philosophy, probably to a religion. Every Society has to act upon dogmas, and dogmas are exactly those things that are most disputable. It puts a man in prison for the dogma of the sanctity of property; it hangs a man for the dogma of the sanctity of human life. [11]

[10] *The Spice of Life and Other Essays*, ed. Dorothy Collins (Beaconsfield, Eng.: Darwen Finlayson, 1964), 114.
[11] *ILN*, March 16, 1907.

Dogma is a frightening word these days. People run from it. Those of us who take our religion seriously, that is, who actually believe our beliefs, are usually told that we need to do away with dogma, which is divisive, and be "inclusive" and "tolerant" so that we can all get along. But the problem is that "inclusiveness" and "tolerance" are dogmas. It is not dogma that divides people. It is dogma that brings people together. The ultimate common bond is truth. That is why it is worth arguing about.

> People talk nowadays of getting rid of dogmas and all agreeing like brethren. But upon what can they agree except upon a common dogma? If you agree you must agree on some statement, if it is only that a cat has four legs. If the dogmas in front of you are false get rid of them; but do not say that you are getting rid of dogmas. Say you are getting rid of lies. If the dogmas are true, what can you do but try to get men to agree with them? [12]

"The dislike of defined dogmas", says Chesterton, "really means a preference for unexamined dogmas." [13] The people who cling to the dogma of tolerance of course do not know that they are dogmatic. And as a matter of fact, their dogma is a bit mushy and vague. But their basic belief is that because there are exceptions, then there are no rules. However, the presence of exceptions, even the allowance of exceptions, is not an argument for tolerance; it is an argument for the rule. And everywhere we look, we can see that the exception proves the rule.

We see it in politics. Democracy, says Chesterton, means "the rule of the rule—the rule of the rule over the exception." [14] Democracy means that most of the people are right

---

[12] *DN*, February 13, 1906.
[13] *Charles Dickens, CW* 15:163.
[14] *Utopia of Usurers, CW* 5:491.

most of the time. Sometimes the majority of people can be wrong about something, but they eventually discover that they cannot sustain the error. Chesterton says that he sometimes found himself in the minority on a particular issue, in which case he appealed not only to reason but to tradition, where the "Democracy of Dead" generally can be counted on to vote for what is right. In any case, says Chesterton, "all rule rests on the divine hunger in all the hearts of men; and that there is still a common conscience which is the thing by which we erect institutions and accept creeds, even if at times whole tracts of humanity can be sunk in special ignorance or swept away with special delusions." [15]

We see it in economics. Wealth is an exception. So is poverty. The rule is that people should be able to be sustained by honest work. Economics is about bread and not about money. But we have seen the middleman, the trader, rise not merely from being the exception to being the rule, but he has become the ruler.

We see it in art and literature, as well as in life. Tragedies are exceptions. We can avoid them, we can fear them, but they happen, and we have to deal with them, rather than letting them deal with us.

We see it in religion and the supernatural. Miracles are exceptions. We can pray for miracles, we can hope for miracles, but we cannot expect miracles. If miracles were not wonders, they would not be miracles.

We see it in education, in the blessed duty of teaching our children the truth. Whether at home or at school, we can recognize the rule and even more easily recognize the exception. The exception is usually used to discredit rather than to affirm the rule. The authority of the family is being undermined by the state because the state does not grasp

[15] *DN*, January 21, 1911.

the concept of the exception proving the rule. The state, which must only intervene in families under abnormal circumstances, is increasingly interfering with the normal.

> Common-sense, the oldest thing in history, has put all children under the authority of their parents. It does this for two unanswerable reasons. First, that to let a child alone is to murder it. Second, that Nature has inspired two unpaid persons with a fantastic taste for taking care of it. But common-sense also says that there are exceptions; and that when the two persons are blood-drinkers or devil-worshippers, or have a taste in torture, the children should be taken away and the child-torturers very severely punished. I do not wonder they were severely punished; I can imagine them savagely punished. . . . Such hatred of one's own flesh has in it something mysterious and unfathomably shameful; and starts alive that same nerve of loathing that leaped back from witchcraft or that cries aloud at sexual perversion. Nothing, one would think, could be simpler or saner than that the tribe should make an example of such demoniac abusers of the family. Democracy is right when it stands for the normal; not when it stands for the average.[16]

We see it in the family. When the world is ready to overturn the institution of marriage in order to accommodate a small percentage of people given to a particular perversion, and when those who speak out against such a total loss of common sense can be convicted and imprisoned for "hate speech", then the exception has become the rule and we are living under the dictatorship of relativism.

We have to rely on the Church's teachings to get us back to what is normal and to be able to grasp once again that paradoxical proverb that the exception proves the rule. "When we are rid of the modern nightmare, of the mad

[16] *DN*, February 25, 1911.

locking up the sane and the exceptions ruling the rule, there remains the true philosophic problem of the extent to which the rule can allow for the exceptions." [17]

Finally, there is one other way in which the exception proves the rule. It has to do with an exceptional writer who keeps proving that the rule is right, who defends the ordinary, who speaks up for the normal, who says what is true when the truth is exactly what we need to hear, who pulls everything together when the world seems to insist on tearing everything apart, who simply speaks common sense when no one else dares utter it. G. K. Chesterton is exceptional. But he proves the rule.

[17] *New Witness*, August 8, 1919.

APPENDIX

Chesterton vs. Darrow

One of the defining moments of the twentieth century was the Scopes Monkey Trial in 1925. It is usually invoked to represent the triumph of reason, progress, liberty, and all those good things, over superstition, backwardness, constraint, and all those bad things. Also included on the list is the triumph of science over religion. But what it represents is hardly what it was.

The trial itself was a charade, staged mostly for the press and for the economic benefit of Dayton, Tennessee, with two gigantic figures of American law and politics descending on the tiny town and representing the two sides: famed criminal lawyer Clarence Darrow and former secretary of state and presidential runner-up William Jennings Bryan. John T. Scopes, a physical education instructor who never actually taught evolution, was approached by the American Civil Liberties Union (ACLU) and agreed to help them run a test case of Tennessee law that at that time forbade the teaching of evolution. Scopes agreed to play the role of pawn after other teachers, including the principal of the school, had turned down the ACLU's offer of, not immunity, but immortality.

The trial was rife with paradox. Although the man supposedly on trial was Scopes, it was actually Fundamentalism that was on trial. Although Scopes technically was found guilty, the teaching of evolution was vindicated. Although Darrow, who was defending Scopes, technically lost his case, he was hugely successful in his scathing attack on Fundamentalism. And although Bryan, representing the prosecution and the state, won, in the course of the trial he literally found himself on the witness stand defending a literal interpretation of Genesis, and in the process, indicting Fundamentalism and humiliating himself. He collapsed and died a week after the trial ended.

The consensus is that Darrow obliterated Bryan, a consensus helped along by accounts in the press written by the acerbic columnist and curmudgeon H. L. Mencken.

Detached objectivity was not Mencken's strongpoint. He actually met with Darrow and other lawyers from the ACLU before the trial and helped them strategize. According to his memoirs, Mencken told them "getting Scopes acquitted would be worth a day's headlines in the newspapers, and then no more, but smearing Bryan would be good for a long while." [1] After Scopes was found guilty of teaching evolution and fined one hundred dollars, Mencken's paper paid the fine.

In addition to the paradox that the winners were the losers and vice versa, within a generation, the theory of evolution emerged from the muck, fully formed, and devoured its former rival. Consequently, the new and unquestioned precept was that no secular classroom may play host to a biology lesson that taught that the universe or life or mankind had a divine origin. Darwin had gone to the head of the class, and the Creator, sometimes known as God, was expelled from school altogether.

And still another paradox was that at the same time of the Scopes Trial, a huge Fundamentalist revival was sweeping the country led by the likes of the fire-and-brimstone

---

[1] H. L. Mencken, *Thirty-Five Years of Newspaper Work: A Memoir by H. L. Mencken* (Baltimore: Johns Hopkins University Press, 1994), 136.

preacher Billy Sunday. Where Fundamentalism was losing ground in the classroom and courtroom, it was gaining ground on the popular level wherever it pitched its tent across America, creating a huge disconnect that still exists in this country, where both the media and the academic establishment do not represent what the majority of people think and believe.

It was paradoxical, which is why it caught the attention of a journalist on the other side of the Atlantic who was well acquainted with paradox. Writing at the conclusion of the trial, he already understood the mythical proportions that the Monkey Trial had reached. He duly noted that the journalists had had their joke, that the "small American towns which are least ready to preach evolution (i.e., the survival of the fittest) are most ready to practice it",[2] and that it seemed a strange format in which to try to settle the question, that in fact the question was not settled, and that the press seemed much too eager to attack the Bible and to swallow Darwin, or, to choose to be on the side of the monkeys as opposed to on the side of the angels.

But he also pointed out a thornier, more practical problem that continues to plague public education though the press and the politicians and the courts continue to dance around the issue with acrobatic aplomb. "It is the great paradox of the modern world," he wrote,

> ... the fact that at the very time when the world decided that people should not be coerced about their form of religion, it also decided that they should be coerced about their form of education. ... It is obviously unfair and unreasonable that secular education should forbid one man to say a religion is true and allow another man to say it is untrue. It is obviously essential to justice that unsectarian education

[2] *ILN*, August 1, 1925.

should cut both ways; and that if the orthodox must cut out the statement that man has a divine origin, the materialist must cut the statement that he has a wholly and exclusively bestial origin.[3]

The journalist was Gilbert Keith Chesterton, writing in the *Illustrated London News*.

Chesterton was a fearless controversialist, taking the side of tradition against fashion, orthodoxy against modernity. He publicly debated the leading secularists of his time: George Bernard Shaw, H. G. Wells, Bertrand Russell—and, eventually, Clarence Darrow.

In the years following the Scopes Trial, Darrow was not in the courtroom much. He had found a new, lucrative career when he discovered people would pay to see him argue. Mencken, after dining one evening with Darrow in 1930, noted in his dairy, "Darrow roves the country engaging in debates on religion, and is said to make a lot of money."[4]

Will Rogers warned prospective opponents, "Don't anybody debate with Darrow. He will make a monkey out of any opponent. He hadn't been in Tennessee two weeks till he had the entire state jumping on the backs of chairs, picking flees off each other."[5]

When Chesterton came to America in the fall of 1930 to be a guest lecturer at Notre Dame, he received invitations to give talks all around the country. After leaving South Bend, Indiana, he conducted a brief lecture tour, which was shortened due to his wife's poor health. Lee Keedick, who served as Chesterton's agent in setting up his lectures,

---

[3] *ILN*, August 8, 1925.

[4] H. L. Mencken, *A Diary of H. L. Mencken* (New York: Knopf, 1989), 7.

[5] Irving Stone, *Clarence Darrow for the Defense* (New York: Doubleday, 1949), 493–94.

arranged for Darrow to debate Chesterton in January of 1931 in New York City. The debate was held in the city's grand hall, the Mecca Temple, and the hall was filled to its four-thousand-seat capacity for the occasion.

The announced topic of the debate was "Will the World Return to Religion?" which Chesterton argued in the affirmative, Darrow in the negative. Unfortunately, no transcript was made of the debate, but from the contemporary accounts, as well as from the writings by each man on the topics at hand, it is possible to get a glimpse of what occurred that night, as well as to reconstruct their respective positions in such a debate.[6]

Darrow led off the debate stating that people prefer reason to superstition. Chesterton responded that he agreed with every word Darrow said. It was a typical technique of Chesterton always to begin a debate by agreeing with something his opponent said. It not only established common ground, but it threw the opponent off guard, as it did the shocked Darrow.

Chesterton argued that people are indeed reasonable—usually. And that is precisely why they embrace a religious understanding of existence and will always continue to do so. Humanity is not complete without religion. If the opponents of religion try to do away with it, if religion is suppressed, suffering results. But anyone who tries to suppress religion will fail. It would be as if some austere sect tried to suppress laughter.

Darrow argued that the religious idea is based on crude and uninformed theories of the universe. There is less religion, less supernaturalism every year. Mankind has moved

---

[6] In addition to the sources listed below, the re-creation of the debate was derived from a report of an eyewitness account given in 1953, by a Father Madigan, who was a professor at Marquette University and was also in the audience at the 1931 debate.

beyond religion, and to return to it would be a backward step. He sardonically attacked the Genesis creation account, as he had done at the Scopes Trial, pointing out how simplistic and contradictory it was.

Chesterton responded that he did not know whether Darrow was debating with him or with "some Fundamentalist maiden aunt". Chesterton, a Roman Catholic convert, drew a distinction between the way Catholics and some Protestants interpret Scripture. There is such a thing as allegory and symbol and parable. "Whether or not the garden was an allegory, the truth can be very well allegorized as a garden. And the point of the allegory is this: Man, whatever else he is, is certainly not merely one of the plants of the garden or one of the animals of the garden. He is something else, something strange and solitary."

The distinction was lost on Darrow. He wanted to keep focusing on the topic of evolution.

Chesterton pointed out that Darwin's missing link is still missing. If there were a missing link in a real chain, it would not be called a chain at all. Evolution, as an explanation of the cause of all living things, is still faced with the problem of producing rabbits out of an empty hat, a process commonly involving some hint of design.

Darrow wanted to know if Chesterton rejected science. Did he believe in miracles?

Chesterton said that one does not have to reject science to believe in miracles. It is science that confirms that miracles are miracles. Most normal people believe in miracles. But believing in miracles does not make it easy to believe in them. That is why they are called miracles. "The most unbelievable thing about miracles is that they happen."

Darrow thundered, "Science disproves the miracles which organized religion asks us to believe! And everyone knows it!"

Chesterton calmly responded, "Everyone doesn't know it. The most scientific and critical investigators have the greatest difficulty in explaining such modern miracles as the cures at Lourdes. The modern world swarms with miracles. If you say they are not reported and testified to, not alleged to occur, I say you are a baby in the knowledge of the modern world."

When Darrow tried to argue that science had more authority than religion, something remarkable happened. The microphones stopped working. Darrow stopped talking, waiting for the technicians to fix them. Chesterton shouted jovially, "Science you see is not infallible!" and the audience roared with laughter.

One of the things that Darrow took great pride in was his agnosticism. Chesterton, however, pointed out that "agnostic" is simply the Greek word for the Latin word "ignorant". Darrow insisted that the definition of the word "agnostic" is that of a doubter. Everyone is an agnostic to the beliefs or creeds he does not accept.

Chesterton said the doubter does not accept any definitions. And the skeptic never thinks he is wrong. He never thinks that there is *any* wrong. But neither does he think there is any right. If he is sincere in his skepticism, he really cannot think at all. Because thinking involves accepting certain things—things that cannot be proved but can only be accepted—on faith. All thinking begins with assumptions that cannot be proved. In logic, we call these axioms. But the real skeptic has nowhere to begin because he must doubt everything. And so he sinks through floor after floor of a bottomless universe. Reason can only be built on faith, and that faith is the foundation of our civilization.

Darrow maintained that the origin of what we call civilization is not due to religion but to skepticism. The modern world is the child of doubt and inquiry, as the ancient world was the child of fear and faith. And the man of the modern world is far too clever to believe in the claims of religion.

Chesterton said that whenever he hears of a man too clever to believe, it is like hearing of a nail that is too good to hold down a carpet, or a bolt that is too strong to keep a door shut. What is man? Thomas Carlyle defined man as an animal who makes tools, but ants and beavers and many other animals make tools, in the sense that they make an apparatus. No, man is much better defined as an animal that makes dogmas.

Darrow accused religion, especially the Roman Catholic Church, of always being opposed to scientific progress and to the growth of knowledge.

Chesterton explained that the whole history of the Catholic Church is one long guardianship of learning and knowledge, from the days when the monasteries preserved all the existing science and learning, until modern times. It was the Church that gave the modern world its hospitals and universities and paved the way for the discoveries boasted by modern science, because the Church has always defended reason. "These things have been going on all sides, and everybody has heard of them except Mr. Darrow."

The audience was stunned.

One eyewitness, who said she had gone into the debate fearing for Chesterton because of Darrow's reputation for annihilating his opponents, was shocked to find out how the two compared. Next to Chesterton, she said, Darrow "appears positively muddle-headed".[7] Another observer said, "It was billed as the 'Clash of the Titans,' but only one Titan showed up."

[7] Cyril Clemens, ed., *Chesterton as Seen by His Contemporaries* (Webster Groves, Mo.: International Mark Twain Society, 1939), 66–68.

Reporting on the debate in *The Nation*, Henry Hazlitt wrote:

> Mr. Chesterton's argument was like Mr. Chesterton, amiable, courteous, jolly; it was always clever, it was full of nice turns of expression, and altogether a very adroit exhibition by one of the world's ablest intellectual fencing masters and one of its most charming gentlemen. Mr. Darrow's personality, by contrast, seemed rather colorless, and certainly very dour. His attitude seemed almost surly; he slurred his words; the rise and fall of his voice was sometimes heavily melodramatic and his argument was conducted on an amazingly low intellectual level.[8]

Darrow's tendency in the debate was to make one extravagant, unsubstantiated assertion after another about the authority and accomplishments of science. Chesterton showed the inherent problems of science being the new authority: "So far the result would painfully appear to be that whereas men in the earlier times said unscientific things with the vagueness of gossip and legend, they now say unscientific things with the plainness and the certainty of science."

In the debate Darrow also demonstrated his ignorance, not only about religion, but about history and science as well. He said that an atom was the same thing as an electron. He didn't know anything about Mendel's law of heredity, but simply assumed it was wrong because it contradicted Darwin, and besides, Mendel was a Catholic monk.

In his account of the debate, Hazlitt wrote, "Ostensibly the defender of science against Mr. Chesterton, [Darrow] obviously knew much less science than Mr. Chesterton did; when he essayed to answer his opponent on the views of

[8] Henry Hazlitt, "Debate", *The Nation*, February 4, 1931.

Eddington and Jeans, it was patent that he had not the remotest conception of what the new physics was all about."[9]

Commenting afterwards on the debate, Chesterton said, "When I tried to talk about Greek cults or Asiatic asceticism, Darrow appeared unable to think about anything except Jonah and the Whale."

"When it was over," reminisced one person who saw the debate, "everyone just sat there, not wishing to leave. They were loath to let the light die!"[10] A vote was taken at the Mecca, and the audience, by an almost three-to-one margin, said Chesterton had won the debate.

Wrote Hazlitt,

> [Darrow's] victory over Mr. Bryan at Dayton had been too cheap and easy; he remembered it not wisely but too well. His arguments are still the arguments of village atheists of the Ingersoll period; at Mecca Temple he still seemed to be trying to shock and convince yokels. Mr. Chesterton's deportment was irreproachable, but I am sure that he was secretly unhappy. He had been on the platform many times against George Bernard Shaw. This opponent could not extend his powers. He was not getting his exercise.[11]

Whereas William Jennings Bryan was something of a blunderbuss and full of himself, certainly an easy target for Darrow or anyone else, Chesterton was self-effacing and witty and charming. While his graceful rhetoric and logic were nearly unequaled, it was Chesterton's humility that utterly disarmed all his adversaries. H. G. Wells, whose ideas on just about everything were challenged by Chesterton, hated the fact that, try as he might, he could never get

[9] Ibid.
[10] Clemens, *Chesterton as Seen by His Contemporaries*, 66–68.
[11] Hazlitt, "Debate".

mad at the man. Chesterton once wrote, "This virtue of humility, while being practical enough to win battles, will always be paradoxical enough to puzzle pedants."[12]

Chesterton continues to puzzle pedants—and pundits. They do not quite know what to do with him. The current strategy is to try to ignore him. This may answer the question about why we still hear so much about Darrow's victory at the Scopes Trial and so little about his defeat at the hands of Chesterton. Two of the three main biographies of Darrow do not even mention the debate with Chesterton; the third treats it as a minor embarrassment.

And where was Mencken all this time? He never once mentioned the debate in all his voluminous writings, nor did he ever seriously attempt to grapple with Chesterton's ideas. His attitude toward Chesterton was contradictory at best. In print he once called him "the cleverest man in all the world",[13] but in private correspondence called him "one of my pet idiots".[14]

Perhaps the reason Mencken and others who knew about the debate were silent about it is that they find it convenient to ignore the Chesterton business because he unsettles questions that they insist are settled. We do not wish to admit that there are still two sides to the debate between science and religion, that, in fact, the real debate is not between science and religion but between materialism and Christianity. We do not have the intellectual energy to grapple with the paradox that would allow both science and religion to stake their claims, or the even more profound paradox that faith and reason do not contradict one another. Instead we ban the issue of divine origin in the name of

---

[12] *Heretics*, *CW* 1:130.
[13] H. L. Mencken, *Smart Set*, January 1910.
[14] H. L. Mencken, *Letters of H. L. Mencken* (New York: Knopf, 1961), 165.

academic freedom and stubbornly ignore the natural implications of a purely "natural" explanation of the universe, of
life, and of that by-product we call civilization.

According to legend, Clarence Darrow said at the time
of the Scopes Trial, "It is bigotry to teach only one view of
origins." It is a quote his critics like to repeat, and his defenders wish to deny. If he did not really say it, however, it is to
his discredit that he did not. In any case, Chesterton really
did say, "Bigotry is an incapacity to conceive seriously the
alternative to a proposition." [15]

The reason why Chesterton was a superior debater—and
thinker—to Darrow and to others is that he truly understood both sides of an argument, an art that is all but lost in
most of today's debates, which are nothing but quarrels, or
shouting matches conducted in sound bites. Chesterton could
state his opponent's side usually better than could the opponent himself. Darrow perhaps would have been better prepared for the debate if he had read the *New York Times* a
few weeks earlier, where Chesterton wrote that the "stronger
skeptic" challenges the believer thusly:

> What are your judgments but the incurable twist and
> bias of your particular heredity and accidental environ-
> ment? What can we know about judgments except that
> they must all be equally unjust? For they are all equally
> conditioned by defects and individual ignorances, all of them
> different and none of them distinguishable; for there exists
> no single man so sane and separate as to be able to dis-
> tinguish them justly. Why should your conscience be any
> more reliable than your rotting teeth or your quite special
> defect of eyesight? [16]

But Chesterton also had a reply for his own challenge:

[15] *Lunacy and Letters* (London: Sheed and Ward, 1958), 151.
[16] *New York Times*, December 28, 1930.

It may be incredible that one creed is the truth and the others are relatively false; but it is not only incredible but also intolerable that there is no truth either in or out of creeds and all are equally false. For nobody can ever set anything right if everybody is equally wrong.[17]

But at the time Darrow should have been in New York reading the newspaper, he was instead in Washington, D.C., speaking to a group of seven hundred black students at Howard University and making the astonishing comment that they should not believe in God because "if there is a God, *He is white,* and therefore unfriendly to the colored race." [18] A banner moment, no doubt, in the history of religion and race relations.

It is ironic that Darrow was known throughout his career for defending "unrestricted freedom of expression", yet he always attacked those who expressed religious beliefs. Darrow's aggressive agnosticism only served to narrow public debate rather than to broaden it. Chesterton not only found Darrow's stance predictable; he also understood its consequences. Doubt does not build anything; it only destroys. This is Clarence Darrow's sad legacy, which Chesterton described in prophetic words: "Religious liberty might be supposed to mean that everybody is free to discuss religion. In practice it means that hardly anybody is allowed to mention it." [19]

[17] Ibid.

[18] Michael Hogan, "Darrow vs. Chesterton", *Truth Magazine* (repr., Brooklyn: International Catholic Truth Society, 1931). Tract reprinted from *Truth Magazine.*

[19] *Autobiography, CW* 16:225.